20 MUST ASK QUESTIONS®
for every
PROPERTY
INVESTOR

MARGARET LOMAS

First edition published by John Wiley & Sons Australia, Ltd in 2009. This edition, fully revised, updated and expanded, published in 2019 by Major Street Publishing. PO Box 106, Highett, Vic. 3190 E: info@majorstreet.com.au W: majorstreet.com.au M: +61 421 707 983

© Margaret Lomas 2019

Quantity sales. Special discounts are available on quantity purchases by corporations, associations and others. For details, contact Lesley Williams using the contact details above.

Individual sales. Major Street publications are available through most bookstores. They can also be ordered directly from Major Street's online bookstore at www.majorstreet.com.au.

Orders for university textbook/course adoption use. For orders of this nature, please contact Lesley Williams using the contact details above.

The moral rights of the author have been asserted.

A catalogue record for this book is available from the National Library of Australia

ISBN: 978-0-6484795-4-3

Cover design by Simone Geary
Internal design by Production Works
Printed in Australia by Ovato, an Accredited ISO AS/NZS 14001:2004 Environmental Management System Printer.
10 9 8 7 6 5 4 3 2 1

Disclaimer: The material in this publication is in the nature of general comment only, and neither purports nor intends to be advice. Readers should not act on the basis of any matter in this publication without considering (and if appropriate taking) professional advice with due regard to their own particular circumstances. The author and publisher expressly disclaim all and any liability to any person, whether a purchaser of this publication or not, in respect of anything and the consequences of anything done or omitted to be done by any such person in reliance, whether whole or partial, upon the whole or any part of the contents of this publication.

CONTENTS

PART III: OTHER ESSENTIAL INFORMATION

ABOUT THE AUTHOR

Margaret Lomas hosted two weekly property investment shows on Sky News Business Channel 602: 'Your Money Your Call' and 'Property Success with Margaret Lomas', which she created and produced. She now hosts 'Property Investing Matters' on the web TV channel, My Property TV.

She is the bestselling author of eight property investment books, including titles such as *20 Must Ask Questions® for Every Property Investor, Investing in the Right Property Now!* and her book *How to Achieve Property Success,* which is the update and compilation of her first three bestselling books.

Margaret is also the founder and a director of Destiny® Financial Solutions, a company which assists people to acquire successful property portfolios through comprehensive education, advice, support and mentoring, and finance setup and structuring. She is the past chair and current board member of the Property Investment Professionals of Australia (PIPA) and past board member of the Real Estate Institute of NSW (REINSW), Business Central Coast and the Small Business Development Corporation of NSW. She is a Telstra NSW Business Woman of the Year and Westpac Business Owner of the Year recipient and was voted one of Australia's 100 Women of Influence in 2015.

Margaret is a qualified financial adviser and investment property adviser and a Senior Associate with FINSIA, the Financial Services Institute of Australasia.

ACKNOWLEDGEMENTS

Writing a book can be a mammoth task, and when you are also trying to operate a business and be there for your family, it is something that is impossible without support and input from so many people.

The team at Destiny® is a strong and committed group of people who help Reuben and I bring alive the dream of assisting as many people as possible to achieve their financial goals through property investing. We are blessed to have so many people to share our vision, and I thank every one of them. My beautiful children are all grown up and three have children of their own. They are dynamic adults and support me every day. Mark, Kristy, Belinda, Michael and Rebecca (and their amazing partners) – I love you all so much.

Reuben continues to shine for me through thick and thin. Never has a man given so much of himself for the dreams of his partner. His commitment is breathtaking, and every day I am thankful for his presence in my life.

FOREWORD BY NEIL JENMAN

Australia's trusted real estate consumer advocate

Being a consumer advocate has its drawbacks. And no, it's not the abuse or threats from crooks that bother me most (although my wife might disagree). What bothers me, no, what *really upsets* me is seeing the damage done to so many decent and trusting folk. If people saw what I see – what really goes on in the property investment industry – they'd never go near property again.

In all the years that I have been helping consumers make good real estate decisions, I have seen the devastating impact of so many bad decisions. The worst, the ones that upset me most, are the older folk, those from, say, their mid-50s up. At that age, if you lose your money, you seldom recover.

It's bad enough if you have spent your life partying and neglected to save and invest for your future retirement, the so-called 'golden years', but it's far worse for those who *have* worked hard, diligently saved and invested their savings, only to then dive into the property ocean and get torn apart by some of the thousands of sharks that infest this ocean. If I count bad advice – which can be just as financially devastating as crooked advice – I *conservatively* estimate that 80 per cent of advice given to today's property investors is not just useless, it's down-right dangerous.

I have seen people lose their life's savings. I have seen elderly folk lose every cent – even their family home. And, worst of all, is the emotional damage these people suffer. It's heartbreaking. Many commit suicide, so strong is the combination of shame at what they feel was their stupidity and their rabid fear of a future being both old and poor. Theirs are the stories that have affected me the most.

As Robert Daley, the police officer turned author once wrote: *'My heart has been broken a thousand times. I've got scar tissue on my soul.'* That's me when I think of what I have seen in the property industry, especially the investment industry.

I get great joy out of helping consumers who contact me *before* they do anything in their real estate lives. I love showing home sellers – in less than 60 seconds – how auctions are the worst way to sell their home. I love showing home buyers how they can save tens of thousands of dollars by asking seven simple questions. Best of all, I love the appreciation I get from sellers and buyers. Even though I can't help everyone, I try. So, please, if you are selling, buying or investing, get good advice *before* you make a major decision. I'll always find a way to help you. Try me.

When it comes to investing in property, however, there is one piece of advice I always give – study Margaret Lomas. Read her books and articles, watch her on TV, hang on her every word.

I have never met anyone in the real estate investing world more trustworthy than Margaret Lomas. She has no vested interests. She makes no money no matter where you buy or what you buy. She is fiercely independent. She is honest to a fault.

I repeat: I constantly give three words of advice when I am contacted by property investors: *study Margaret Lomas.* That's it – three simple, but oh-so incredibly powerful words that, if followed, will virtually guarantee you cannot lose when you invest in property. On the contrary, now that you have this wonderful book in your hands, *20 Must Ask Questions*® *for every Property Investor*, you should be able to do what you have always wanted to do when you have thought about investing in property: make a decent profit, either with the rental income from that property or its capital growth – or both.

This book is great value and I urge you to read it and study it and then put Margaret's 20 powerful questions to work to help you and your family build a better life.

I hope you never make a bad investment decision as a result of bad advice from sharks who made tens or hundreds of thousands of dollars profit from you. I have been bitten badly fighting some sharks. It's bad for my health, I assure you. Just ask my wife what we have suffered – often together – in the fight to rescue investors from sharks.

Margaret Lomas is not a shark. If I was allowed only one word to describe her, I would choose *angel*. Yes, Margaret truly is the Angel of Property Investing.

If you want to contact me when you're selling or buying a family home, please do. But when it comes to investing, I am going to tell you what I am telling you now, *study Margaret Lomas*. You can't go wrong if you follow these 20 Questions and the advice that goes with them.

Now, a final word of great caution: I know most people don't read books. The common excuse is, *'I don't have time to read.'* Well, consider this: it takes one minute to read one page. This book is about 225 pages. It will take you fewer than four hours to read – and what will you get? You will get knowledge that will protect you and, quite possibly, set you up financially for life. But, if you don't make the time to read it, then, I am sorry, but you are almost certainly going to live the rest of your life regretting that you did not do the one smart thing I asked you to do before you invested in real estate. Again, I repeat: *study Margaret Lomas*.

Finally, by way of disclosure: Margaret Lomas and her husband, Reuben, are close friends with me and my wife, Reiden.

We both agree that we have no friends we trust more. I am proud and honoured that Margaret has allowed me to write this foreword to her brilliant book.

Safe investing to you.

Neil Jenman
Jenman – Real Estate Support you can trust
Jenman.com.au
1800 1800 18

— *Part I* —

INTRODUCTION

— Chapter One —

THEY CALL ME LUCKY

IT'S NOW BEEN almost 10 years since I wrote the first edition of *20 Must Ask Questions® for Every Property Investor.* Since then those questions have become the staple for property investors all over Australia, as well as in many other parts of the world where property investing is popular. Answering these questions reveals the critical fundamentals of a property, and tells investors whether it will be a viable investment.

For more than 20 years now I have been involved in every forum available for property investors, written hundreds of articles, hosted my own TV shows, created educational courses and recorded podcasts and video blogs. I receive dozens of questions and comments every single week, which I do my best to answer. Perhaps the most common question I am asked is one about specific areas. 'What do you think the growth is going to be like in this place?' or 'Should I buy in that area?' Equally, at seminars and expos, people always want to know specifics about areas, and most investors want someone whom they perceive as being an expert to tell them where to buy next.

I've often been heard saying that I don't have a crystal ball, and I think that property advisers who categorically state that particular areas are going to perform really well at a future date are taking a pretty big risk. Even though I have travelled the country extensively for my TV shows, interviewing mayors and reviewing areas, I cannot possibly know about every single area in Australia – or the world for that matter, since this book is equally appropriate in all countries – so it is a little unfair to expect me to be able to roll out stats and information on demand! Also, even if I *do* have valid and current information about an area that I and others perceive to be a good opportunity, it is likely that by the time you ask me about it you will already be too late to take advantage of that information. With property everywhere, there's typically quite a short window of buying opportunity before that location is discovered and mined to the point that it is too late, for a while at least, to buy there.

Whenever I talk to property investors today and ask them how they are picking areas to invest in, it's usually via magazines, online forums or tips from experts at seminars. The important thing to note about this is that, if you are hearing about an area from others, or reading about it in the popular press, then you've missed the opportunity to buy there. By the time you get back to your home and begin your search, most of the good buys will be under contract, prices will have begun to rise and the cost to you of entering that market will be much greater than if you had found it a few months earlier. If you are being told about an area by a spruiker at an expo or workshop, or via a glossy brochure, it is most likely because they want to sell you property there!

So, many years ago I developed the 20 Questions because I wanted to create a benchmark by which investors could measure the *future* potential of an area, rather than invest based on what is happening at this moment in time. In this new edition of the book, I have updated them – tweaked them a little, added a few new questions and ensured they still have relevance in today's market, which has changed dramatically since I first wrote the questions!

Just as when I first wrote them, these questions will equip you with all you need to be the person who discovers the next best area in which to buy property. As investors, we tend to find out what others are doing, we read magazine, newspaper and online articles and follow the crowd in terms of where we look. This means that, at any one time, many of the property investors in this country, who read the same things that you do, are looking in the same areas as you are. This could result in two possible outcomes. On one hand, a 'false' demand could inflate prices temporarily in that area and create a kind of 'insider trading' situation – enough people talking and writing about a suburb or town results in short-term demand and lack of supply, with prices rising unsustainably. In months to come, after the frenzy is over, the market returns to normal and you find yourself with a property worth less than you paid. On the other hand, where the area has legitimate characteristics, which confirm that buying there is a good idea, once you have heard about it too many people have already entered that market and you will have to pay more and more to get the same rent returns that the lucky people who were 'first in' get. How much better would it be for you, the investor, to always be the first in?

Many years ago I was the co-host of a real estate show aired on my local radio station. One day my co-host proclaimed me to be the luckiest investor he had ever met. When I asked him why, he said, 'You always seem to buy in areas I have never heard of and then, hey presto, six months later everyone is talking about them or writing about them and the areas boom!' While he believed this to be luck, the reality is that I simply always use the 20 Must Ask Questions® to uncover viable areas before anyone else. If I hear about an area, or know of frenzied buying in a suburb or town, I go somewhere else. I make it my mission to track down and seek out areas that no-one has ever heard of or thought of investing in, and see how they stack up against my 20 Questions. If an area does qualify, I believe it has every chance of experiencing long-term sustainable growth and giving me a solid and reliable return.

Investing successfully is not about huge growth, although when that happens to a property you buy, you'll be very happy! It's also not about amazing property in romantic seaside suburbs or other iconic areas. Buying well doesn't mean only ever buying within 10 km of a CBD, where your yields can sometimes be so low that the growth you get cripples you financially along the way. It doesn't involve asking experts what they think, second-guessing the state of the economy or finding areas with incredible rental returns.

Investing successfully is about understanding the everyday, bread-and-butter characteristics of a sound property investment. It is about being able to confirm sustainable rental demand, strong intrinsic growth indicators and internal economic vibrancy. And all you need to be able to find out these things are the answers to the 20 Must Ask Questions®!

This book will not cover the very lengthy process you need to undertake after you have answered the questions – I have written plenty of other books to help you with financing and buying property, structuring ownership, managing your property and your portfolio, and so on (see details at the back of this book). It will not provide basic education for the new property investor, nor give lengthy explanations of cash flow, growth and taxation, although all three are referred to in this book and used in many of its examples. Each of my previous books has an important place in the education process, and a significant relevance to people at every phase of their investing life, from novices to highly skilled investors.

This book will, however, increase your chances of getting it right once you are ready to buy property! It will minimise your risk and maximise your chances of buying the right property, by providing absolute minimum standards to apply when choosing your next property. By asking each and every one of these 20 Questions, you will have covered all the important research and left no stone unturned. While there can never be any guarantees, the chance of you buying a lemon will be as small as it could possibly be.

So read on, enjoy the book, and take comfort in the knowledge that you will never have to rely on the opinion of anyone else again about where to buy. You may just become someone other people call 'lucky'!

— *Chapter Two* —

PROPERTY YIELDS

FOR AS LONG as I have been a property investor, and advising others to become one, I have had a single, unwavering message: buying property which has the best possible cash flow that you can achieve (while not ignoring the potential to grow) is generally better for you as an investor than buying purely for growth.

Saying this doesn't mean that I subscribe to the theory that you must choose between the two. Our own portfolio of properties is absolute proof that choosing cash flow as your main motivator when selecting property doesn't preclude you from also achieving good growth. I believe that our portfolio has grown as well as most properties in this country today. Some of our properties have grown really well, some have had average growth and one or two were even lemons, which we eventually disposed of. Could we have done better? Yes, most likely, but to do so would have required us to take risks that we simply weren't prepared to take at the time, due to many circumstances including the fact that we were in our own business (and that means you never really have an assured income) and we were raising five children! Feeding them was a priority.

When we bought those properties, we didn't specifically choose them for their growth potential, but the research we did, using the 20 Questions, certainly ensured that we ultimately achieved it (sometimes by a great degree, and others by only a small degree), while all the time the cash flow we were receiving meant that our personal budgets were not strained as we waited for that growth.

If you're listening to the 'experts' these days and trying to educate yourself, give no credence to the theories that property with a solid cash flow won't grow in value. In my own personal experience, that's absolute rubbish. People who tell you this are probably the same people who are trying to sell you property in what they call 'high-growth areas' and what I prefer to call 'high-profit' areas (high profits for them, that is, when they sell it to you). What you will learn as you read this book is that you can't tell ahead of time whether an area will be high growth or low growth. You can, however, learn how to establish whether there's a strong chance of growth *at some time* in the future.

The simple facts are some properties grow well and some grow less well, and before you buy you can hunt down the indicators for growth just as easily as you can find out the population numbers and what the median price of property is in the area. Another important fact to know is that properties that *do* grow well don't have to be situated in capital cities, and they do not have to have low yields (that is, a low-rental return for the price you are paying), which is typically the case in most larger cities. You can find out more about this and read a thorough explanation of the different types of growth later in this book, after I present the 20 Must Ask Questions®.

What I want you to know now, before we get into the 20 Questions, is that if you seek out property in areas that, based on history, everyone *knows* will grow – usually because they are smack in the middle of a capital city or are very large regional areas – it is most likely that your yields will be low and result in a huge difference between what comes in (rents) and what goes out (expenses). The difference will be so great that your tax breaks (the tax you get back because you claim both the actual loss and the on-paper loss from any depreciation you might be entitled to) will only make a small dent in it. The rest, I am sorry to inform you, will come straight from your hip pocket. You may feel that you can afford to pay this difference, but you must identify how many times and for how long, because that will determine how many properties you can buy.

The reason for this is because areas known as 'blue chip' are mostly places which were *former* hotspots. At some time in recent history, it was likely that these were areas that had affordable prices and lots of potential. It might have been an area which bordered a favoured area but which was relatively cheaper. It could have been a suburb which was less than desirable and had a different demographic than it now has. At some point over the years it became more popular, and those demographics changed. Prices went up and, as demand for property grew, people held onto what they owned, reducing supply. There were fewer rentals and the demand continued to grow. As more and more property was built further and further away from the central part of that area, the ones closer in gained in popularity. People who bought into the area in the early days did so because it satisfied the criteria that my 20 Questions cover. Now, while the area still maintains the fundamentals, it has grown to be way past affordable, and the relative yields are likely to have become very low. Blue chip areas are only good to invest in if you can find them before they become blue chip areas!

While I don't believe that cash flow and growth are mutually exclusive, I do know from history that, generally speaking, property with high growth may have low yields and, generally speaking, property with higher yields may have lower growth (although history has shown us that this is not always the case). In the following chapter, I will examine why this is. Please be aware, however, that in both categories there will be exceptions. This book will show you how to have a greater chance of buying one of those exceptions – as my husband and I have done, many times.

Before you move on to learn any of that, though, it is important that you understand how cash flows on an investment property. A complete explanation of cash flow can be found in my book *How to Achieve Property Success*, but here is a really quick refresher. For those of you who are new to positive cash flow, it should make things a little clearer.

HOW CASH FLOWS ON PROPERTY

The aim you have when you buy property as an investment is both to see an increase to the value of that property over time, and to achieve an income via rents. The amount of rent you receive in relation to how much you have paid for a property will depend on many things – the demand in the area for properties like yours, the desirability of your property in relation to others in the area, the interest rates of the day if you have borrowed to buy, and many other factors.

In some areas, property prices are very high because a lot of people want to buy them – perhaps due to their proximity to services, the perception of the area by others, the limited availability of new land to build more residences and the high number of homebuyers in that area. In other areas, property prices are much lower because not as many people want to buy them – they might be a long way from services and employment, or there may be more renters and an abundance of vacant land for new building being released in the area.

Rental returns do not tend to have such a great disparity. While it certainly costs more to rent in some areas than others, the fact that wages are linked to the economy means that the rental return variance from area to area, town to town and state to state is not quite as great as the variance in purchase prices.

What this means is that in some areas you can get more return for your purchasing dollar, week to week, than you can in other areas. Investors hope that eventually, when they liquidate their assets (i.e. sell their property), the property in the more sought-after areas (despite its lower yields and relatively poor cash flow week to week) will reap a bigger reward in terms of growth than the higher-yield, cheaper property. While this may make sense, you will see later that this has not necessarily always proven to be the case.

As well as receiving weekly, monthly or quarterly rent on a property, it will have expenses that you must pay week to week. Firstly, there is the interest that you pay on any loan that you obtain to buy the property. Even if you contribute a deposit of cash and the amount you finance is consequently less, the opportunity cost of not earning interest on that cash should be considered an investing expense. In addition to the interest on your loan, you will pay owners' corporation fees if applicable, rates, repairs, insurance and taxes and any number of other expenses.

GEARING AND TAX

Before we take a look at how you make money from owning property, we need to first consider the tax treatment of any investment in property that you might make. While taxation benefits should never be the reason that you invest in property, gaining a tax benefit can help you to meet any shortfall that may be created where expenses exceed income, especially in the early years where these tax benefits are likely to be the greatest.

'Gearing' is a term which refers to borrowing to buy an investment. Gearing allows you to leverage the smaller amount of cash (or property equity) that you may have by adding a loan to it and increasing your purchasing power.

In Australia, the term gearing has become increasingly synonymous with property, and the term 'negative gearing' has now been adopted to describe investing in property. However, this is a bit misleading because it makes it sound as if borrowing to buy property is a negative thing, when it doesn't have to be.

All countries have differing rules around the tax benefits, if any, you can claim when you invest in property. In Australia, any shortfall between income and expenses can be claimed against the tax that you have paid on income elsewhere (at the time of writing). Other countries will have their own rules around the tax treatment of rental income – for example, in the US any rental income losses can only be written off against other passive income. Some other countries carry forward any rental losses to write off against future rental profits.

Here is a brief synopsis of how differing systems may work. Bear in mind that, at any time, your country may change the rules around what they allow you to claim and how you can claim it, so it is useful to understand how the different models may work.

Claiming against any other income

In this system, any loss that you make on a property you own can be claimed against any other income you have earned, in the year you have made the loss. So, for example, if you own a property where the expenses exceed the income by, say, $2,000, this $2,000 reduces the taxable income you have earned overall in the year. If you earned $50,000 from your job, for example, you would only have to pay tax on $48,000. If you presently pay tax at 30 per cent, then you would pay $600 less tax in this scenario.

Claiming against other passive income

In these circumstances, any loss that you make on your property investment can only be written off against income made on other types of investments or on other property. The calculations used in the section above are the same, except that the only income which can be reduced by the loss is income from shares, bank deposits, bonds and other financial instruments.

In countries where this system applies, any unused loss may or may not be carried forward, as per the section following.

Carrying forward losses each year

Under this arrangement, any losses you make on a property in one year carry forward to the following year. These losses keep accumulating until one of two things happen – either the property begins to make a profit (in which case you begin to use the carried forward losses to write off this profit, until there are no more losses to write off) or you sell the property, in which case, in countries where capital gains tax is charged on property gains, you would offset this gain with the remaining carried forward losses to create a situation where less tax is paid.

So, for example, say your property made that same $2,000 loss in one year. You would carry forward this loss to the next year. In that year, the property may make an $1,800 loss (assuming the rents increased). The accumulated losses are now $3,800. The following year, there is a $1,600 loss. Accumulated losses are now $5,400.

Fast forward a number of years, and the rents have risen, which is usually the case with most properties. You reach a year where, instead of a loss, you receive $200 more income than expenses. You write off this profit with some of those accumulated losses. Each year as the rents rise and your profits become greater, you write them off, until there are no more carried forward losses to use. It is at that stage that you would begin to pay tax on the profits.

If you sell before you have used up the carried forward losses, the residual amount is deducted from any capital gain made upon sale, and in those countries where capital gains tax is charged, that tax will be less.

Carrying forward losses until sale

Where you are not allowed to offset your losses against any gains made in future years, the entire carried forward loss is quarantined to be offset against future capital gains upon sale. This loss may or may not be allowed to be written off against gains made on other property or other investments on which you might realise a gain along the way, or it may only be allowed to be written off against the gain made against the property on which the losses were incurred.

In countries where capital gains tax is charged, this loss is then offset against that gain to reduce the amount of capital gains tax paid.

Other taxes and systems

There are such a wide variety of approaches to property investing around the world (too many to list here). Before you begin to invest it is critical that you completely understand the system in the country in which you are investing.

Some countries allow foreign investors to buy their property, and in those countries there are at times different rules for those investors than there are for residents. Some countries have a straight yearly tax on gross rental income (for example 25 per cent in Canada), with previously paid taxes able to be reclaimed if the property incurs a loss after considering allowable deductions. Capital gains tax, where it is charged, is calculated in many different ways, with some countries allowing an exemption for any time that a property was a principal place of residence. Most countries allow property investors to reduce the tax they pay on rental income by first deducting many (or all) of the expenses of holding that property. Some countries, like France, have an overall wealth tax, which is an amount levied upon your total property worth once it exceeds a threshold. In Australia, there is land tax, which is state based and levied on the total amount of land you own in any one state, once a threshold is reached.

As you can see, there are many ways you can be taxed, and many benefits that you can also receive, once you know about them. Make your very first job as a property investor to become educated about what your country allows, so that you can be in the very best position before you begin.

POSITIVE OR NEGATIVE CASH FLOW?

After collecting the rent and paying out all of the property expenses, some properties will have a shortfall, others will meet their own costs while others still will make a profit, where the income exceeds the expenses. For those investors who are buying rental properties in countries where you are allowed to write off any rental losses against other income, the extent to which those losses can be written off is limited to the marginal tax bracket that you are presently in and to the rules of that country. For example, if you pay 30 per cent in tax, and your country allows you to recover property losses by claiming them against other income, you will recover 30 per cent of the loss. The rest (70 per cent) is borne by you. If you still have a loss after this tax is refunded, your property has a negative cash flow.

Here is a brief example of how this might work:

Rental income	$25,000 per annum
Property expenses	$28,000 per annum
Gross loss	$3,000
Tax return on this loss	$900
Net loss	$2,100 (paid by investor from own funds)

You may wonder why you would buy a property for which you have to reach into your own pocket, every week or month. The simple answer is that people accept a negative cash flow because they think that once they are ready to sell they will reap more in capital gain than they have paid each week to hold the property. While this may indeed be the case, it also may not, and the investor could instead be seriously out of pocket and facing significant investment losses. In addition, every property with a negative cash flow that an investor accepting continual negative cash flow buys, impacts directly on their lifestyle today. As I mentioned earlier, you must consider how much disposable income you have and are willing to commit to this strategy, as this will instantly determine how many properties you can buy. You must also be aware that any negative movements in the economy, such as rising interest rates, will make your negative cash flow *more* negative. You might be able to afford the $100 or so per week that you have calculated will be your negative cash flow today, but if rates rise and it becomes, say, $150 a week, could you still afford it? If you also have a personal mortgage that rises at the same time, a rate rise may really hurt you financially. This, combined with inflation and the low wage growth which has been evident in recent years in many countries, means you might even be forced to sell before the anticipated growth has occurred. You're then left with no capacity to recoup what you have lost.

On the other hand, but equally risky, is the situation where you find property with exceptional rental returns. In this scenario, you may actually receive more rent than you need to cover your expenses – and this provides you with a positive cash flow. You will pay tax on this positive cash flow because your net profits will be considered income. Properties with these extremely high returns often exist in areas where there is a reason for the rents to be so high – for example, there may be a single industry in the town, like mining, which means there are a lot of renters who are there for the employment. Areas such as these carry high risk of volatile values – and in Australia during the mining boom there were many examples of people paying high prices for property with unbelievable returns, only to have the values fall alarmingly as the demand for commodities lessened.

For investors who are not willing to take either of these risks, the properties to look for are those situated in ordinary residential areas in both cities and regional towns. They tend to have rental yields of around 5 to 6 per cent of the purchase price. It is at this level of rent return that the better cash flow outcomes can be achieved. Properties closer to the central business district can have yields as low as 2 to 3 per cent, and this can make achieving an even or positive cash flow very hard indeed.

It's important to point out here that, over time, your negative cash flow property may *become* positive cash flow. If rents rise in the area, the percentage yield you are achieving rises, as it is measured against whatever you paid for the property, not what it is worth in the coming years. If you buy a negative cash flow property and rents quickly rise, then you may not have to bear that negative cash flow too long. However, if they don't rise, or if they were relatively low to begin with, you may sit on that negative cash flow for a long time, effectively compounding your losses and placing more reliance on exceptional capital growth to pay you back.

HELPING WITH THE CASH FLOW

I have already mentioned that a negative cash flow property may indeed grow well and provide a significant return in the form of capital gain at some time in the future, but that staying in the market while you wait for the growth may be difficult. I also said that positive cash flow property which is the result of exceptional yields may carry an added risk, since the rents are likely to be high for a reason, such as the area being volatile. In the olden days, areas based on one industry had incredible yields, because everyone wanted to rent from a relatively small pool of available property. These types of areas were well 'mined' (excuse the pun) by investors, causing unprecedented growth in values. Many of these same areas sent speculative investors broke, when the work dried up and the rents fell. Those same investors couldn't find tenants, couldn't sell, and values also plummeted.

Areas can come into and out of positive cash flow as their yields in relation to values go up and down. If an area has a boom and values rise sharply, it can take time for rents to begin to move. New investors to those areas will bear a negative cash flow until such times as the rents start to rise with inflation and demand. As long as you use the 20 Questions to buy in such an area, the long-term prognosis should be a good one. In the meantime, there are two things you can do to make your cash flows a little more palatable: learn more about on-paper deductions and learn how to pick properties where the negative cash flows will be short-lived.

ON-PAPER DEDUCTIONS

Positive cash flow property has a raw rental return greater than expenses (meaning that you likely will pay tax on that gain), and negative cash flow property has a negative cash flow because the expenses exceed the rental income, meaning you will get a tax refund in those countries which allow rental losses to be written off against other active or passive income.

In many countries where tax advantages are provided to property investors (such as Australia, the US, Canada, UK and New Zealand to name a few) you are also allowed to claim the 'loss of value' of the building and any structural improvements which have been made, and in some countries on fixtures and fittings within your income-producing property. While every country differs as to the rates allowed and the period over which they can be claimed, they are all similar in that they allow a percentage (for example, 2.5 per cent in Australia) of the original value of that building (or fixtures and fittings in some countries) to be claimed every year until the item is written down to zero (in Australia, this would be 40 years from the original date of construction). Here is an example:

Joshua paid $350,000 for a property with an original construction cost of $250,000. He can claim 2.5 per cent of the construction cost ($6,250) every year for 40 years.

Joshua receives $330 a week rental return or $17,160 a year. His costs are $19,000 for the year (interest and property costs).

His actual loss is $1,840, on which he receives a tax break of $552 (as he pays tax at 30 per cent). This tax break partially offsets his loss, but he still has a shortfall of $1,288.

Joshua can also claim the loss of value on the building for that year of $6,250 (which is 2.5 per cent of the original construction cost), at 30 per cent tax rate ($1,875).

Joshua now gets a total of $2,427 of his tax paid on other income back ($1,875 plus $552). Since his actual loss was only $1,840, after the tax break Joshua is now ahead by $587 for the year.

Knowing about on-paper deductions, how they are calculated and how to determine how much to allow for them in your calculations *before* you buy is very important for an investor in any country. It means that, even though a property may look like it is going to give you a net loss (according to its price and rent return), it may actually provide an after-tax profit once the depreciation claims are made. It also means that two properties that seem similar in price and rent return can have a very different cash flow, depending on their original construction costs and what can be claimed within the building itself. If one property has had structural improvements or is newer than another, not only is it likely to attract a small increment in rent over its neighbour, it is also likely to bring greater deductions and therefore better cash flow.

Once you comprehend this concept you will appreciate that whether a property is cash flow positive or not is determined by much more than just its rental return. When we begin to discuss the 20 Must Ask Questions®, I will explain more fully how you can use this knowledge to uncover more opportunities. You will see that positive cash flow properties are all around you, if you just know how to find them!

CHOOSING PROPERTIES WITH SHORT-LIVED NEGATIVE CASH FLOW

When you ask the 20 Must Ask Questions®, you will uncover areas and properties with exceptional potential for the future. Some of these properties will be in areas that have had (or are in the process of having) a price boom, or at the very least a healthy increase. You will discover, once you know more about the 20 Questions, that price booms in such areas are less about investor sentiment than they are about characteristics in the areas that bode well for the future. Usually, prices increase first and rental returns follow more slowly.

It could be, though, that you discover an area that has all of the characteristics of a great future hotspot, but the rental returns are a little low and the cash flows are a little negative as a result. While I still firmly believe that positive cash flow property is crucial in order to build a large portfolio, I would like to clarify the following:

All investors should work towards having a positive cash flow portfolio as soon as they possibly can. This may mean a short-term negative cash flow on some properties, but only where the area satisfies every one of the 20 Must Ask Questions® and appears to be undervalued in terms of rental return at the present time.

I have written that in both italics and bold, so that you know that I am saying it to you very loudly and firmly. I am *not* saying that it is now okay to buy negatively geared property because you believe that you must accept a negative outcome to buy in 'good' areas.

What I *am* saying is that if it appears that an area has all the right characteristics, as defined by the 20 Questions, if it has recently undergone a price increase, is in demand from renters (i.e. has low vacancy rates) and if rental returns haven't moved very much at all in the past two or three years, then it is likely properties there will be positive cash flow soon, once the rents catch up. The 20 Questions should reveal if there is evidence rents will rise because of the demand and vibrancy in the area.

You must, however, ask yourself:

- Can I afford the negative cash flow for the short term? Build in a margin on the time that it might take for rents to rise, so you can be sure you can afford to support that shortfall for as long as you need to.

- Do local property managers believe I will be able to raise rents incrementally over the next few lease periods? You should be able to speak to someone who has a good handle on the market and who can tell if vacancy is decreasing.

- Is there anything I can do in the meantime to impact on rental returns? Small and inexpensive enhancements may allow you to increase the rent. For example, in hot climates the addition of an air conditioner might cost $1,500 (which if you borrowed to make the purchase would add $130 a year to your interest expenses), but might bring $10 a week ($520 a year) in additional rent and some extra cash flow as you depreciate the air conditioner.

- How low a price can I buy the property for? Find out as much as you can about the vendor so you can ascertain the price they need to sell and negotiate accordingly. I have secured amazing bargains through negotiation that have resulted in a positive cash flow immediately, when I had thought it would be a few years away. Positive cash flow property is still the most viable way to build a sound and sustainable portfolio. Ideally, achieving this cash flow upon settlement is the best outcome, as then you can afford to buy a greater number of properties. If this is not possible, though, consider properties with small negative cash flows if evidence exists that this situation will change in the very near future. Aim for a portfolio that becomes positive cash flow as quickly as possible and remains that way.

At the back of this book you can find details of how to access a calculator which can work out for you how long a property is likely to remain negative cash flow. It makes for a great planning tool!

Accepting a small negative cash flow that may be quickly turned around might be better than not buying until the market improves. In my experience, well-bought property rarely goes backward in value (although economic conditions can cause any property to stagnate for a while), so staying out of the market may be a greater mistake than getting into a market with a small weekly outlay.

— *Chapter Three* —

BALANCING THE CASH FLOW AND THE GROWTH

THE IDEAL SITUATION is, of course, to buy a property that will not only skyrocket in value, but also provide a positive cash flow for as long as you hold it, so that your lifestyle is not affected. This perfect scenario is not very likely to occur for most people, but a prudent investor can learn how to thoroughly research and buy properties and improve their outcomes. These properties can then support themselves over the years through rents and possible tax breaks, until such time as the investor needs to use the equity – which hopefully will have grown somewhat – for their retirement needs. This equity may then be used in a number of ways: by liquidating the portfolio and having cash available for superannuation, annuities or other investment vehicles, or by having enough equity (because the portfolio has grown well) that the positive cash flow is enough alone to fund your chosen lifestyle.

As I said in the previous chapter, it isn't *impossible* to find property that provides both cash flow and capital gain over time, despite what the self-proclaimed experts (you know, those 'advisers' who are selling property to you) would have you believe.

However, you must follow certain rules, be unemotional and put a huge amount of effort into the task. Property investing is not a get-rich-quick scheme, and you should run very fast from anyone spruiking any kind of strategy that presents it as such.

In our own property portfolio, my husband and I have many properties that have had positive cash flow and that have also grown exceptionally well in value. The more property you buy, the greater the chance that you will acquire some exceptional performers, both in terms of growth over time and cash flow every week. However, if you consider property investing subjectively, and remember that *generally speaking* a property may have more of one than the other, sometimes you must make an initial choice between buying for the chance of good growth and buying with the aim of acquiring cash flow, in those early years at least.

The two options tend to be seen as at odds with each other. Die-hard growth investors would never consider investing in a property for any other reason than to make a gain on its value. Investors needing to make ends meet in their personal lives, by contrast, seek property that requires no commitment from their own pocket. However, let's take a look at the two options and how they can be used in your own investing life.

CAPITAL GROWTH

If your aim is to obtain the highest capital gain possible, you would most likely invest in cities where you believe that prices are booming.

A good example is the larger markets of Sydney, Los Angeles, London, Auckland and Vancouver. The past few years have seen exceptional growth in all of these cities and if you timed it well, you would have made some great gains. However, there are three important things to note:

1. The rental yield in these cities is low, in most cases well below 3 per cent, and buy-in prices are very high – over $1m median in some cities. The weekly cash flow shortfall to hold such a property as an investor is huge. Very few property investors, who typically are median wage earners, could afford to hold a property in these areas while they wait for that growth.

2. Booms often come on the back of a protracted period of very low growth. Sydney, for example, grew by around 17 per cent for the entire seven years prior to the start of the boom of 2013– 2017. If your timing had dictated that you bought at the commencement of that seven-year period of low growth, then the growth experienced in the booming four years that followed represented 'catch up' growth. If you had sold just before that boom, then your actual return on investment would have been very poor indeed.

3. Many properties in these cities have since been affected by a downturn, with some higher-end property falling by as much as 20 per cent. This sudden, 'bubble' type growth can often result in sharp falls and it can be hard to work out when that will happen, so you can be in danger of losing a significant portion of any growth you obtained if you hold too long.

It certainly seems like an excellent idea to run out and buy property in areas where prices are rising now and with a high expectation of short-term growth. The problem for investors is that prices tend to rise far more quickly than rental returns. It's typical for a property situated in a booming area to rise by 20 to 30 per cent, but it is likely that rental return will rise only with inflation, increasing by around 3 per cent per annum. Eventually, rental returns may catch up with values, restoring the balance, but this can take many, many years. So, if you bought property after the values had started to increase, but before the rental returns moved, you are likely to be supporting a sizeable negative cash flow. While you wait for the rental returns to grow, you must make up the difference between income and expenses where the property is geared (that is, you have borrowed to buy it).

The issues here can be many, for example:

- Your lifestyle is impacted as you use funds previously available for personal spending to support the property.

- Your ability to buy multiple properties is limited by the amount of surplus cash flow you have from your employment (which will decrease with each purchase).

- You are taking a gamble – what will happen if you commit your personal funds but the anticipated growth does not occur, or you are too late, as many were in the closing stages of that Sydney boom?

There are, of course, a number of benefits too, including:

- You may well realise a good or even exceptional gain upon eventual liquidation.

- You may be able to take advantage of the fast-growing equity to leverage into more and more property, as long as you have the disposable income to support additional purchases without suffering financial hardship.

Growth on property is an excellent way to augment your retirement income. It is not guaranteed, however. We simply do not live in a world where property increases are perpetual and never-ending despite many property spruikers claiming that property doubles every eight to ten years. We have come through some exceptional times for property all over the world, but it always comes to an abrupt end with little warning. Any dream run must come to an end and, if this occurs just after you employ a negative cash flow strategy for your property investing, you may well suffer hardships you did not expect.

CASH FLOW

You now know the different ways that cash flows on a property purchased as an investment, and the differing tax regimes that might be applicable in the country where you are buying property. You can see that cash flow on a property is dependent on many things – the rent return you receive, the tax system in your country, the amount of money you earn and at what marginal rate you pay tax on that income, and whether depreciation benefits apply.

From all of this information you can see that it isn't as simple as just finding a property either in an area that seems like it will grow really well, or in one where the rent returns are significant enough to be able to cover the expenses you will incur when holding property there. You can also see that property with both a good cash flow *and* the capacity to grow well for the period that you intend to hold it isn't impossible to achieve.

I want to once again reiterate, though, that it can be a mistake to focus purely on cash flow alone, because this is likely to lead you into choosing property in areas with good yields, but no chance of good growth. While it can be tempting to get a high rental yield, the downside risk of that is too great.

Remember, properties with these high rental yields usually exist in areas where one industry supports the town, and as such there is a demand for rentals while that industry exists. These areas usually enjoy normal inflation of rental returns (and often higher if there is a particular and sudden demand for rentals, say when that one industry expands or has a product or commodity which is in demand) and, sometimes, short-term high demand from investors keen to get in for those high yields. This short-term demand pushes up prices and creates a false reading on the demand factor.

This is all very well if you can buy in while it's cheap and ride the boom upward, then sell just before that boom stops (which would coincide with when that single industry suffers the downturn, which happens frequently). The thing is, though, that unlike a share which can be traded almost instantly, property just doesn't turn around that quickly, and usually by the time you become aware that the dream run might be over, the downturn in the economy comes immediately. Demand dries up very quickly and you may just as rapidly ride the downfall as you did the boom.

Even if there is no great boom in prices, and all you get is a good rental yield, your ultimate goal may not be met. When you buy property, your aim is to have it pay for itself while you hold it and create a capital value gain big enough to give you a nest egg when you sell it. If all it does is cover its costs while you hold it, you will have little to show for the exercise once your predetermined investing period ends.

Therefore, *maximising* the cash flows using the knowledge I have given you about how cash flows on a property, and using these 20 Questions to buy property which *also* has the best chance of growing, is the critical balance you need to strike to have a successful portfolio.

The other benefit to investors in purchasing property for cash flow (with attention to growth factors) is that there may be less of a limit on the number of properties they can acquire. If no, or little, personal cash input is required to meet expenses, then an investor will only be limited by their borrowing power and, to some extent, to the equity in their existing property. They will not 'hit the wall' in terms of how much they can afford to personally contribute to the investment portfolio. The drawback, of course, *may* be said to be the lower growth – at the point of sale, the portfolio of a cash flow investor may be worth less than that of a growth investor, assuming that the growth investor has been able to afford to continually support the negative cash flow of their portfolio. A more likely scenario is that the cash flow investor will have a higher net worth than the growth investor, as they will have been able to buy more properties.

It is also a fact that, as long as you hold properties over a longer term, many areas with good cash flow have consistent levels of growth which occur year in and year out. Adelaide is a great example of this – over a 20-year period its growth figure for the entire 20 years is often very similar to the more volatile Sydney and Melbourne, with Sydney and Melbourne getting higher rates of growth in patches but longer periods of little or no growth. This then means that your investing period becomes a critical consideration too – those with longer periods before they need to sell can buy in areas with lower, but often more consistent, growth.

WHICH SHOULD YOU CHOOSE?

As a financial adviser, I am often asked to take part in debates about which is the better investment: shares or property? While I will take part in them for the amusement factor (they can be fun if you don't take them seriously), I believe that it's not possible or even fair to compare the two. To do so equitably you need to weight each asset class (and each asset type within the class) by its risk factor and consider costs, tax benefits, rental return, dividends and a whole host of factors which make the two very different. Since the risk factor is impossible to measure using any easy mathematical formula, it is better to accept that these two classes behave differently, and it's more prudent to view a potential investment in terms of its appropriateness for your personal circumstances than to compare one against the other.

The same is true of pure growth investing versus pure cash flow investing. Many investors purchase property solely for its ability to deliver a profit over the short or medium term. These investors buy according to their beliefs and hopes about the potential future gain, with an exit strategy firmly in place and knowing the time period in which they would like to invest and divest. They accept that they will have to fund negative cash flows while they wait for those gains to come. The methods growth investors use when buying property number in the dozens – from individuals second-guessing the market by estimating possible future values, right through to purchasers of 'off-the-plan' developments and amateur renovators employing a 'buy-to-improve-and-sell' strategy to make a quick profit. The one thing all of these investors have in common is the level of risk they take – their purchase success is based purely on future events that may or may not occur. Property in any one area rarely follows 'trends' – so an investor is usually unable to use historical performances in an area to predict future behaviour.

When an investor buys for cash flow, it is usually because they lack the ability to cover any losses each week, no matter how small the commitment or how great the promise of good capital gain. Buying for cash flow usually allows an investor to buy more properties, although this can be limited by equity if all properties chosen deliver lower than average capital growth and the investor had low equity to begin with. The main risk is that the investor may need to sell before the anticipated time, but even under these circumstances it is less likely the investor will actually make any loss – the investment simply won't make as much profit as they would have liked. There is also the risk, of course, that the rules around property investing and its tax treatment may change and that some tax advantages will no longer apply. However, in this event, most property investors are likely to feel some impact, regardless of their original motivation for making the purchase, and the playing field would be relatively level in this respect at least.

In my opinion, your aim should always be to find the property which has the best possible chance of growth for the highest possible cash flow you can achieve. From there, you can adjust this according to your circumstances. If you lack strong personal cash flows, err on the side of finding good cash flow property, but don't forget that it needs to grow too. The reverse is true for those with tons of personal cash flow but little in the way of property equity – you need to err on the side of choosing areas with signs they are about to grow now, but don't lose sight of your cash flow needs.

The following examples will help you to appreciate the most likely outcome of each method of investing.

Example 1

John is an investor heavily weighted in one city market. He has bought property to make large amounts of money from capital gain and so felt the need to remain in capital cities. As John's own home was worth $600,000, and he owed only $100,000 on this property, he had enough equity to buy seven properties altogether, keeping his borrowing exposure to under 80 per cent of his total property values (but borrowing all of the purchase price plus costs of his investment properties).

After five years the total value of his portfolio (not including his own home) is $5.14 million. The combined original price of each property was $3.5 million (each purchased at different times over a two-year period), and so far he has seen an 8 per cent per annum gain. Based on the original purchase prices, John's rental yields are an average of 4.5 per cent (being 3.5 per cent when originally bought), or $157,500 a year. In addition, John paid $175,000 in purchasing costs, which he funded with his bank loans (making the total loan for investment purposes $3,675,000).

His costs are:

$154,350 – interest-only loan @ 4.2 per cent

$52,500 in costs for the seven properties

$206,850 total

Less $157,500 income

Equals $49,350 a year gross loss

As John has $120,000 a year in personal income, he receives back tax of approximately $14,805 for this loss at 30 per cent.

As a net figure, John pays $34,545 from his pocket each year to fund this loss (gross loss, less tax back).

The immediate problem for John, of course, is the impact of these purchases on his personal cash flow. While he has clearly experienced good gain on these properties, the commitment required to keep them is crippling him financially. Last year he was forced to refinance the properties to provide him with extra cash to fund this loss. This, of course, added to his yearly ongoing expenses and has only served to make his cash contribution greater than it was last year. It also reduced the equity he had in these properties, giving him, in effect, a neutral equity gain for the year.

If John doesn't go broke from the lack of cash flow (which looks highly likely), he may reach a point in the future where this strategy pays off. If we assume he continues to receive the average 8 per cent per annum capital gain (though this is an unlikely scenario, as this is more than twice the national average yearly gain for most countries), after five more years his portfolio will be valued at $7.55 million. He will owe $3.675 million. If he sells the properties, he grosses $3.875 million. He will pay 2.5 per cent to agents for the sale ($188,750) and capital gains tax of 15 per cent (effectively a tax on half of the gain, in this case considered on only the gross gain less agent's fees, but in reality subject to a number of other considerations). This amounts to

$579,188. In addition we must consider the $34,545 from John's own pocket each year for 10 years. As a net return, John sees $2,761,612.

This is, without question, a good return, but it must be weighted by the risks John was taking. First, it is unlikely that John will make it to year five. With little left over for personal expenses he would have to live very frugally indeed! In reality, it's more likely that the big returns will not be there for John, as he will be forced to sell years before the planned date and well before he sees the benefits of compounding capital growth. We also must consider the impact of rising interest rates on John's financial circumstances. If there were even a minor change to rates, John would be forced to sell.

Another important factor for John to be aware of is the potential growth rate. The 8 per cent per annum he saw in years one to five is higher than the historical average of property over time. If this growth rate slowed in the planned period to, say, an average of 5 per cent per annum (still relatively high), then his gross profit would decrease dramatically. Finally, John is very limited going forward – he is unable to buy any more property as he is vastly overcommitted already.

Let's now consider investors with a greater focus on cash flow.

Example 2

Kristine and Kevin also have a $3.5 million property portfolio. They have purchased in large regional centres and smaller cities, as well as outer capital city suburbs. They have 10 properties with an average purchase price of $350,000.

Kristine and Kevin have a wide range of returns for each of these properties. Some are returning 7 per cent of the purchase price in rent, making them profitable before tax. Others have more normal rental returns of around 5 per cent but good on-paper deductions. On average, Kristine and Kevin have a positive cash flow from each property of $30 per week, or $300 in total. This $30 per week represents the after-tax dollars in their pocket – that is, after all costs, including loan interest, are paid, and after all tax claims are made. Like John, their own home had a value high enough to allow them to borrow the entire purchase price plus costs and still keep their total borrowings below 80 per cent of their total equity.

Kristine and Kevin have the same income as John – $120,000 a year. While they also have a tax reduction due to both on-paper and actual costs, they get back more than they need. In effect, this gives Kristine and Kevin $300 more each week to do with as they wish, since they do not need it to meet any losses they are incurring on their property. Kristine and Kevin are keen to leverage into more property as soon as they can. They understand that the properties they have purchased may have a lower growth rate, so have decided to pour their cash flow back into their loan, and thus create some additional equity.

If we were to assume that Kristine and Kevin only achieve half the growth that John enjoyed (that is, 4 per cent per annum), then after 10 years their investment property portfolio would be worth $5.18 million. Their debt, as a result of the cash flow and of making extra repayments over and above the interest, would then stand at $3.519 million. (I have assumed interest on the whole debt of $3.675 million, as this is what John pays each week, even though the actual interest bill will decrease as more of the repayment pays off the principal, and the positive cash flow will gradually increase.)

Although it is unlikely that Kristine and Kevin would want to sell after 10 years, let's say that they decide to do so. They owe less than John, as they made repayments on the principal of their investment debt using their positive cash flow, so after they sell they make a gross profit of $1,661,000. They pay 3.5 per cent to agents for the sale ($181,300) and capital gains tax of 15 per cent, which totals $221,955. As there has been no input from their pockets each week, we need not consider any further costs to them. Their net gain is $1,257,745.

This is considerably less than John. However, we must consider that, firstly, there is no reason they cannot make it to year 10, as they have no commitment from their own pocket. While John will struggle financially to make ends meet, Kristine and Kevin will not experience any change in lifestyle. In fact, they may well want to commit some of their personal funds (which John does not have, as his funds are financing his loss) to debt repayment as well, to further accelerate debt elimination and increase their net gain. Secondly, they can actually afford to *add* to this portfolio as it increases in value; they may have been able to afford another two or three properties during the 10-year period based solely on their increased equity. Thirdly, cash flow investors usually employ a 'buy and hold' strategy. Kristine and Kevin's goal is to create an income on which they can retire. Ultimately, while growth is important from a leveraging point of view, they never plan to sell for the profits, so the cash flow carries far more weight for them. Finally, what will happen if they do see a better gain than anticipated? It would only take an extra 1.5 to 2 per cent growth across their portfolio to bring them into line with John, without the commensurate amount of risk and negative cash flow.

It is my personal experience that, as long as you spread your investing over many property types and areas, and follow the 20 Questions, you will almost certainly get better-than-national-average capital growth. You can also use the positive cash flow, which should grow as rents grow, to further pay down debt and gain additional equity in your portfolio. By buying for cash flow with an aim to get as good a growth rate as possible without sacrificing that cash flow, you have a good chance of buying a property which just happens to be in what becomes the next hot spot!

SO, WHICH IS BETTER?

Having invested in property for more than 20 years now, and owning a large portfolio of properties, I can tell you what has worked consistently for us. Buying property for its cash flow (while looking out for the signs that there was still potential for growth in the future) allowed us to continue to maintain the lifestyle we have today at a time when we needed it most – while our children were still at home and had countless needs and expenses. Now that they have all flown the coop, we are just as thankful to have properties which look after themselves from a cash flow perspective, and we have built a good amount of personal net worth from the growing values.

If the property you buy has all of the characteristics of a sound investment, it should, at some time in its life and as long as the cash flow is not too negative, begin to return a positive cash flow. The combined effect of repaying debt (and so reducing costs) and raising rents in line with both inflation and with market demand, closes the gap between income and outgoings. The aim is that, by retirement, this gap is not only closed, but you actually make money from the rents each week, as well as from the capital gain. That way, your choice in retirement can be to continue to hold the property (which will continue to grow) or sell to realise the gain. The aim of getting a positive cash flow, or as close as possible, is not to make money today – it is to get you to the point where the property takes care of itself, reaches a point where it grows, and then begins to make money each week from the cash flow and each year from the capital gain. Without positive cash flow, or with a highly negative cash flow property, it is much harder to stay in the market long enough to reach this point.

Never fall into the trap of thinking that one method is more right than the other, however. I often see investors taking part in various online property forums, passionately discussing why their preferred method of investing is better and far more profitable than that of their peers. It seems the discussion always travels the same route. The growth investors think that tax deductions are the icing on the cake and should not distract you from the ultimate prize – capital gain. They energetically apply various complicated formulas and do endless historical research to attempt to anticipate the areas of highest return. They accept sometimes large losses as the cost of investing, believing that the gain in the long run will far outweigh the costs over the short term. And they can be right. It can and does pay off for some. Incredible gains can be made if the market timing is right. Property millionaires are made every year (as are property paupers!).

Meanwhile, cash flow investors swear by their own methods. Many of them have previously been caught out once or twice with negative cash flow property, and they haven't liked the result. Other investors cannot bear parting with cash they can't really afford to lose every week (just to provide a roof over someone else's head), in the hope that, some day, capital gain will make all the pain worth it. So, they commit to never again treading that path, and discover the many benefits of positive cash flow investing including that it can, and often does, grow really well too. Even for those investors whose plunge into positive cash flow property has kept their sale profits down, the safety they have felt, and their ability to maintain a suitable lifestyle today, has been worth the decreased profits.

Investors are not qualified to judge for others which method is right or wrong, as the right method for each investor is a highly personal thing. If you decide to become a property investor (or continue to invest, though differently after you have read this book), you must be guided by both your financial circumstances today, your goals for tomorrow and your attitude to investment risk. It's more about who you are and what you want than it is about what is right or wrong. The method you choose when investing in property should relate to your own personal needs for income and profits, rather than what your best mate is doing or what any property expert recommends.

The following profiles may be of some benefit in assisting you to ascertain your needs.

The growth investor:

- has a short- to medium-term investing period, around five to ten years
- has a considerable excess of income after all personal expenses are met
- is prepared to commit short-term funds to property expenses while waiting for growth
- is comfortable with higher than average risk
- will consider a range of investing options, including higher-risk property in untested areas
- is not fazed by market movements
- is looking to make money from profits and aims to liquidate all property at some time in the medium-term future to provide funds for alternative investing.

The cash flow investor:

- is looking to invest to create an income in retirement from rental return
- has limited surplus income
- cannot afford to commit funds to any shortfall between income and expenses in the shorter term
- has a lower risk profile than the growth investor and is prepared to accept lower growth in return for cash flow
- worries if the market fluctuates too greatly
- wishes to minimise debt as quickly as possible.

There will always be two schools of thought when it comes to property investing, but it is my hope that reading this book leads you to a third school of thought: the cash flow/growth method of investing. The bottom line of this method is that it gives a little both ways – gives up a little growth, and also a little yield, to land in a place where cash flows are sufficient to cover expenses and growth is enough to make the whole exercise profitable.

Whatever you choose, there's work to do, and there's a lot of it! There really is no such thing as a free lunch, and unless you are prepared to carry out your due diligence, you may well be stepping into shark-infested waters with little hope of emerging without at least some small damage. You may even have a whole limb torn off! Don't waste your time trying to justify the position you decide to take. Accept that as investors we are all different and seek differing results for our efforts. Appreciate that both strategies may be right, but only one will be right for you. Always remember, the only wrong strategy is choosing to do nothing. Investing can be fun and profitable, and certainly beats sitting around waiting to win the lotto!

— *Part II* —

THE 20 MUST ASK QUESTIONS®

— *Chapter Four* —

THE 20 MUST ASK QUESTIONS®

YOU ARE NOW at the point where you've learnt about the fundamentals of investing. You should understand a little more about how this whole property thing can work for you, and you also should have explored the rules in your own country, so you know whether it is also going to be a profitable exercise for you.

You're still a long way from being ready to invest, though, and unfortunately, this is the point at which many investors go wrong. They think that just because they know the rules around property investing and how income and expenses are earned and then treated, they are ready to go. They rush out and find a house down the road, or in an area that fits what they think is their price range, and they buy it. Worse still, they hand over all of the responsibility for choosing an investment to the latest magazine property guru, without ever seeing the significant benefit to that guru in having them as a paying client. When I meet investors who own a poorly performing property, you can bet that it is because they decided to become a property investor and either bought whatever they liked the look of, or trusted someone else to pick for them.

This is where the work really starts. If you're not prepared to do this work, then you shouldn't buy property. When you pay someone else tens of thousands of dollars to do it for you, not only do you start the game behind the eight ball, but you learn nothing, and next time you buy you have to pay someone again.

So, let the learning begin as we move on to the most important part of this book – the 20 Must Ask Questions®. As each and every question is of crucial importance to you, I have devoted an entire chapter to each. The questions are not really in a specific order, but nevertheless can be used as an elimination process. By that I mean, when considering an area, if you get negative or unsatisfactory answers to the first few questions, you should stop, eliminate that area and focus on another. That way you can avoid asking the entire 20 Questions and finding, on the last one, that the area doesn't stack up. The process requires a lot of work from you, but not so much work that you'll burn out before you even buy your first or next property!

HOW TO USE THESE QUESTIONS

Though you have decided to become a property investor, it is unlikely that you will quit your job and devote all of your time to the task. Unlike some successful share investments, you cannot realise your gains on property and make a living from them until your portfolio has grown to a substantial size and considerable time has elapsed. This means you will probably be staying right where you are, holding down a regular job and carrying on the business of taking part in life, as you have always done. Because of this, you will also have limited time available.

Unless you buy all of your property in the next street or suburb (which of course is a bad idea, as it means that you are putting all your eggs into the one growth basket), it is unlikely that you will be able to go and look at all the properties that make it on to your final list. It's a nice idea that we could be flying all over the country inspecting possible purchases, but it is neither practical nor necessary.

Hence, the 20 Must Ask Questions®! It's imperative that you use these questions not only to improve the way you buy property, but to enhance the way you search for it and to be more time-efficient in your work. It means that you can vastly reduce the time you need to put into the search for the right area.

As many of you know, I speak at countless seminars and expos. I don't run the kind of workshops where people pay thousands of dollars to get information they could otherwise get for the price of a book. At each event, there are always a number of people who approach me looking like they have just survived a hurricane – tired and dishevelled, with black circles around their eyes and sporting newly greying hair! Their stories of woe generally involve hundreds of hours spent as a slave to their computer, telephone and magazines, as they research area after area only to find that when one area does finally stack up, all the affordable property is under contract and prices have already started to rise. No wonder they end up giving up and paying whatever they need to pay to get someone to do the job for them.

If this is how you're searching for property, you're going to be retired long before your planning for retirement has even commenced! The 20 Must Ask Questions® may be lengthy and somewhat time-consuming, but the way you use them should eliminate areas that were never going to qualify as viable areas in which to invest, long before you spend too much time researching them.

This is the method you should use. If it seems time-consuming in its initial phases, remember it will save you a great deal of time later on. In addition, asking these questions does become a skill that you can get good at – and when that happens, you'll discover that you can find the answers much more quickly because you begin to know exactly where to look and what to look for. This is how to get started:

1. Rather than hearing about an area (from a friend, online or at a course) and then applying the 20 Questions to that area, use a broad area as the starting point. Depending on the size of the country you are in, this could be the entire country! It is acceptable to start by seeing where the experts and magazine are suggesting – but if you do this, try drawing a circle around those areas and looking at ones nearby that may not yet be talked about. Later, these questions will show you how to do that.

2. Work out how much you can afford. To do this, talk to a bank or, better still, a broker like my company that has a deep understanding of property investing. Now, this doesn't mean that, if a bank says you can borrow, say, $600,000, you look for property valued at that price. The future potential of any property is *not* determined by its price, and a higher priced property doesn't mean that it is better. Many people fall into the trap of believing so, but price is not an indicator of future potential. My experience also tells me that the higher priced the property, the lower the yield will be. If you can borrow $600,000, you may consider two properties at, say, $300,000 each rather than one property. This way you can buy in two different areas

and different states. Since property runs in differing cycles all over the country, the ability to spread risk this way is crucial if you are going to get better average growth across the whole portfolio.

3. Contrary to much of what is written about property, I like to look at property in the bottom third to half of an area in terms of price. I have always found that property in these lower price ranges is easier to buy (there are more of them), easier to rent (there are more tenants in this segment of the market) and easier to sell if I am forced to (there are more buyers in this market). The more expensive properties in any area are usually those with features which might suit owner-occupiers and characteristics which add to desirability (but not to value), but these are factors which don't bring about more in rent or greater capital value growth. In fact, it's my experience that, in times of booming prices, cheaper properties (not necessarily the *cheapest*) that meet all of the criteria for intrinsic growth grow faster. This is probably because, as housing starts to become too expensive for the average person, more people look to buy the cheaper properties.

4. Now that you know a little more about the price range you can work with and have decided on a few areas to begin researching, use a real estate search engine, go to each state/territory and enter your search criteria (i.e. areas and price range), then hit 'enter'. Don't just work with one area at a time – work with several, and if you can also choose areas from different states, this will help you to have a more diversified portfolio.

5. You will, of course, get hundreds of responses. Start by eliminating areas based on their population and/or their

proximity to a large city, town or regional area. For example, if the area has less than around 10,000 to 15,000 people, it is likely to be a long way from becoming established enough to experience really good growth. You are also more prone to experience vacancy in a small area like this. However, if that town or area is only 20 to 30 minutes' drive from a city, it should stay on your list for now.

6. You can find out the population simply by typing the name of the area, city or town and the words 'population of' into Google.

7. This process should give you a sizeable list of areas, and hopefully they will be in different states. If your list is one with areas all in one spot, then keep looking as you really need to be making comparisons across many different areas in several different states. If you have done a search like this recently, eliminate any areas about which you have already asked the 20 Questions. However, if it has been some time since you looked into the area, leave it on the list; things can change fairly quickly.

8. Next, for each area, do a quick rental search by finding out for what price properties are renting in that area. You are trying to establish the percentage yield, so that you know if it is worthwhile looking further. Yields below around 3 to 4 per cent will make it very hard for you to see a positive cash flow, even if you do find a property with greater than average depreciation allowances. Areas with yields above 6 per cent can stay on your list for now, but you should quickly determine whether or not they are areas based on one industry and, if so, eliminate them. Keep any properties showing about 4 to 5 per cent yield on your list.

Now you will have a big list, but it will be manageable. If for no other reason than tidiness, sort them into alphabetical order (or state order, or any order you prefer) and start asking the 20 Questions about the first area on your list. As you go through these questions, you'll see that the first 10 relate to the area itself and then once you have narrowed down your areas, the next 10 relate to the properties available in those areas.

By the time you get to Question Seven or Eight, you will know whether to keep asking or whether to move on to the next area and save this one for next time around.

Using this method of elimination, you will achieve a number of things:

- You will no longer be a sheep. You won't be following the crowd around trying to find a needle in a well-searched haystack.

- You will become experienced and efficient in both asking the questions and choosing which areas to question.

- You will begin to develop a feel for the questions that allows you to throw areas off your list quickly – the more you do this, the better skilled you will become.

- You are encouraging yourself to invest more widely. Your search should include many areas, as neither you nor the experts can possibly know all of the areas in enough depth to be able to reliably recommend one or invest in one. You should be learning to invest not only away from your own home, but away from your own state, too! You should also be investing because you found the *best* area out of the whole country, not because you found a good area in the six or so you researched.

When you start your search for your next investment property, you should not have a preference about where it is situated. This is because, if you do, you may well miss something that could have given you a great opportunity. Areas should only be eliminated based on the research that you personally carry out. You must be open-minded and accept that you know nothing about probably 95 per cent of your country.

Our personal clients (those who have used my company Destiny® to help them to invest) have the chance to attend group meetings, where they meet with a peer group and have my guidance. Here they learn more about the practical application of the 20 Questions as well as some important investing skills, such as negotiation. One of the things that we do is to allocate a task to each member of the group, to report on at the next meeting: come back with at least six areas no-one has ever heard of before. I can't tell you the excitement of most of this group when they came back with not only six areas each, but a number that are perfectly viable for investing!

Now that you know how to prepare a manageable list of potential areas, you are ready to begin asking the 20 Questions. In the following pages you will find each of the questions, with as much detail as I could include to assist you to ask them well. Some questions have a lot of detail and take up many pages, while others are short and take up only a few. Don't be fooled: they are all as important as each other!

The first 10 of these 20 Questions are more about area selection than individual property selection. However, since you are often looking at an area because you have come across an actual property first, the last 10 questions address property in general, or an individual property in particular. It's a good idea to try to keep the questions in the suggested order as you ask them – to make sure the area checks out, and then the property within that area, not just the property in isolation.

A final word on the questions and how to use them: each question is part of an entire picture. They are like the pieces of a jigsaw. When you look at a jigsaw puzzle from afar, you won't notice much impediment to the overall picture if one piece is missing. However, look closely at that puzzle, and a missing piece means that you can't get an entire picture. You need all the pieces to create the great looking outcome which is the finished product.

These questions work in concert with each other. The answer to one question will have an impact on the answers to the others. Learning how to be thorough with each and every question will be critical to you painting your own complete property investing picture.

Let's move on to those questions!

QUESTION ONE

What is the cash flow of the area, generally speaking?

Being able to find an area that is not only cash flow positive, neutral or slightly negative, but shows the capacity to grow is, as I have already said many times, the most important feature of how you should be investing. Previously I talked about how some people can handle slightly more negative cash flows while others simply can't invest if the cash flows are anything other than positive.

Whether your needs lean more toward cash flow or growth, the cash flow of the area is an important starting point. Growth investors need an indication of whether the ultimate cash flow is going to be too negative for their budgets to reasonably manage. Cash flow investors need to know if they can actually achieve a positive cash flow or get close enough to it that any negative cash flow will be fairly short-lived.

Determining cash flow is not just about working out the cost of your loan and other associated costs, and then deducting the potential rental return from that figure. As explained in Chapter Two, the ultimate cash flow can be impacted by many things, depending upon the country in which you live and where you invest. It's absolutely imperative that you are able to work out these figures with ease. There is no point in proceeding any further from Question One if you have no hope of achieving the cash flow result you need. You will be disappointed time and time again as you fail to negotiate a price low enough to provide a suitable cash flow. So, commence by following this process.

STEP 1 – DETERMINE RENTAL RETURNS

From Part I you learned how to assess the cash flows of an area, thus you should have an idea of the rental returns for that area. If you keep the area on your list at this stage, it is because you believe that it has potential to have an acceptable cash flow.

For example, a search I undertook while writing this book revealed that Lawnton in Queensland had 63 properties for sale, priced at between $230,000 and $500,000. Within this price range I needed to see rents at a minimum of $220 a week up to at least $480 per week (5 per cent of purchase price) for the property to stay on my list. A rental search on properties which were the equivalent in size and number of bedrooms than those for sale revealed that rental returns were between $270 and $435 per week.

This search also identified something else for me: properties in the lower price ranges have a 6 per cent return while those in the upper ranges start to reduce and return below 4.5 per cent. This supports my earlier assertion: the higher the price, the lower the relative rental yield.

While all properties are negotiable, it is good to know the price band that will give the best return for your dollar. Generally speaking, growth in an area happens widely throughout that area and impacts properties at all levels, although it is often those just below the mid-point in terms of price that do the best in terms of overall percentage growth. Having said that, don't buy such a property for its growth if the yield in that price range is poor, especially if spending less gets you a significantly better yield.

STEP 2 – CONSIDER DEPRECIATION

Next, I would consider what I could reasonably expect to get in terms of depreciation. This is a little harder to determine, and you need to be familiar with the depreciation methods used in the country where you claim your tax benefits.

To complete this calculation, you must make some assumptions. The main one is the possible original construction cost, as most countries base their depreciation benefits on that figure. This will relate to when the property was built and at this early stage of your research it can be hard to find this out.

Remember, this is only Question One. Should a property make it through the entire 20 Questions, there are some checks and balances you will do to clarify that you are indeed buying the right property. Don't worry about being too precise right now, or you will spend many precious hours doing calculations that may have to be redone. It may seem that in this step, you are making a lot of 'guesses'. However, as a property stays on your list for more and more questions, you will be able to check these estimations by asking more specific questions of the agent and the local authorities. For now, the aim is to see if the area, and sample properties contained therein, are *in the ballpark* and therefore worthy of further investigation.

If you are in Australia, Destinylive.com.au has a free to use handy calculator which can help you to establish the potential depreciation allowance. By looking at the pictures of the property provided by the real estate search engine and reading the descriptions, estimate the age of the property as closely as you can. There are some useful websites that have 'sold' data, and these websites will often list not only the size in square metres (or yards) of a property but its original build date.

If you can't find this data for any properties in the area, you will have to estimate, but try to err on the side of caution wherever possible. Then, if you are using the DestinyLive calculator, select the year of estimated construction in the dropdown box. You will also need to enter the approximate floor area, the property type, the nearest major city and the quality of the finish as these elements have an impact on the amount of depreciation you can claim. The calculator will then display an estimate of the yearly building depreciation for you to use.

STEP 3 – IDENTIFY YEARLY EXPENSES

Now you need to know what this property will cost you to hold. This is different than what it will cost you to buy – these expenses are the regular, yearly expenses that you must meet. To identify possible yearly expenses to own this property, you need to include:

- a percentage of the total loan amount that you will need to buy the average property in the area (which is the average purchase price plus your estimated purchasing costs, including charges to convey the property as well as any taxes; usually about 5 per cent of the purchase price), for loan interest – adjust this for the interest rate of the day but do build in a margin by adding 1 to 1.5 per cent to this rate

- yearly local authority taxes, charges and rates

- yearly fees for strata apartments or condominiums

- cost of insurances, including building, contents and landlord's protection insurance

- an amount for repairs and maintenance; say $1,000 per year, more if the property is older

- 10 per cent of the yearly rent for property management fees and associated charges.

STEP 4 – CALCULATE THE CASH FLOW

You are now ready to carry out the calculations. Again, the calculator found at Destinylive.com.au can do this for you, but it is useful to know how they are done. Sometimes I do them quickly in my head if I am in a rush!

1. Add up the total rental return. Use only 50 weeks a year, to allow for changeover of tenants. If the property is subsequently occupied for 52 weeks, this will be a bonus. If you are a risk-averse investor, you might like to allocate four weeks a year vacancy. Be careful though – I have seen procrastinators build in all sorts of additional margins which then make it almost impossible to find property which suits their strict criteria. Often this is a subconscious barrier they are creating so that they don't have to take the leap and become an investor!

2. Subtract from the total rental return the total of your yearly expenses.

3. The resulting figure is your *gross* yearly gain or loss.

If your country does not allow you to claim depreciation, then it stops there. You will either receive a tax deduction equal to your rate of tax if you have a loss, or you will pay tax equal to your present rate of income tax if the resulting figure is a profit. In countries where no benefits are allowed, there may be no tax benefit.

If your country has some form of allowable depreciation, then do this:

1. Use the loss or gain figure from no. 3 and deduct the amount of allowable depreciation that you worked out earlier. The effect will be one of these outcomes:

   • The 'on-paper' loss figure will be greater than the actual loss you are making as a result of the difference between income and expenses;

   • The gain will become an on-paper loss; or

- The gain will be reduced, but will still be a gain. Note that as this 'gain' has been reduced, you may pay less tax on that gain.

  This will depend upon how high your rental yield was in the first place.

2. Multiply this figure by your tax rate. This then becomes the amount of tax you will either get back, or have to pay. Where you have no tax benefits the figure in no. 3 will be the only figure you work with.

3. Add rent to that tax refund. If you have to pay tax, deduct that amount from the rent figure. This gives you the amount of after-tax cash inflow you will get.

4. Deduct the actual expenses you will incur, and then divide the answer by 52, and this will be your weekly cash flow. It will be a negative or a positive number.

Example

Purchase price:	$320,000
Loan to buy:	$336,000 (assuming approximately 5 per cent for purchasing costs)
Yearly rent:	$17,500 (50 weeks @ $350 per week)
Interest costs:	$14,100 loan interest
Yearly expenses:	$4,000 (rates, insurances, repairs, etc.)
Total:	$18,100
Loss:	$600
Less:	$5,500 building depreciation ($220,000 original costs at 2.5 per cent)
Total loss:	$6,100

Tax back on loss @ 30 per cent:	$1,830
Total cash flow in:	$17,500 (rent) + $1,830 = $19,330
Total to pay out:	$18,100
Net gain:	$1,230 or $23.65 a week positive

Note: Your rate of tax will affect this, as will the ownership status – whether you own it alone or with others. If it is lower than 30 per cent, you may not have a positive cash flow. If it is more, you will have a greater positive cash flow.

If this calculation returns a negative amount, you might cross the area off your list or, depending on the amount, you might leave it on. Large negative cash flow properties are very hard to recover from, even where growth is good. This is because you have to see a yearly capital gain of at least the amount of yearly loss to break even, and to make investing in property worthwhile, that capital gain will need to considerably exceed the yearly loss.

However, where that negative amount is small and within your capacity to afford, you would leave the area on the list to see if later questions uncover good potential growth drivers. If this is the case, those growth drivers might be strong enough to push up rents within the first year or two of your ownership. It would be at that point that you would make the decision whether you can afford to fund that loss or if you would prefer to wait until you found something with better cash flows.

Please remember that, at this stage, you have not selected a property. I have shown you an example of how I work out possible cash flows, and to show you that example I have used an actual property found on a real estate website. However, this doesn't mean that I will buy that property. It was used solely for the purpose of establishing a snapshot of what I *could* buy, to see if I wanted to keep that area on my list. I may have to do this exercise a number of times to adequately establish that positive or very close to positive cash flow is actually possible, and that I am not wasting my time moving on to the other 19 questions.

Of course, I may end up buying the property or properties found for my example, but it doesn't matter if they are no longer available by the time I have concluded my research. While good buys do not last forever, as long as you don't spend too much time deliberating over your research, the facts that these questions are designed to uncover will be long lasting. You have time to research well. Just because you have found a property at this stage that looks good and stacks up in terms of cash flow doesn't mean that you have to rush in and buy it before someone else does. If the area qualifies under most of the 20 Questions, there will be other similar properties available to buy. Remember, 'fools rush in where wise men never go'. A wise investor will make sure this is the area to go to before making a move.

Understanding the cash flow is about so much more than simply considering the income and the outgo. You must take into account all of your allowable deductions, your ability to impact in the short term on actual rental returns, the ability of the area to deliver strong growth over time and your capacity to negotiate well. Where you have uncovered an area that has not yet become popular, your choices will be greater and your ability to negotiate enhanced, as there will be fewer buyers in the area. Once the cat has been let out of the bag and the area starts to come under the scrutiny of many investors, properties may achieve full purchase price, though more often than not they don't.

AFTER YOU HAVE ASKED THE OTHER 19 QUESTIONS

You start by asking Question One, and then you later return to ask it again once you have selected an area in which you have definitely decided to buy. Remember, at this stage you uncovered a couple of examples of property in the area. It is likely there will be more. Once you are satisfied that most (or all) of the 20 criteria can be met, you will be ready to return to this question and do some more specific calculations about cash flow.

At the end of the 20 Questions, I have listed in detail some additional information which is important to you. Once you have read it, and have narrowed down your choices to a few properties in which you are interested, return to this question and do the following:

1. Contact the agent selling the property and ask them to give you more specifics. You want to know:

    • the exact age of the property, if known
    • the general condition – ask for up-to-date pictures which haven't been touched up and are not professional shots
    • if any major repair work is needed
    • the number of bedrooms, and so on
    • an estimate of the size of the property (in m²)
    • details about the vendors: Why are they selling? How long have they had this property on the market with that agent and any other agent? Have they committed to buy elsewhere? This gives you an idea of your capacity to negotiate a lower price.

2. Go back and re-establish the depreciation, if allowed, from this additional information. Re-do all of the calculations. If you are in Australia can use the free calculator at Destinylive.com.au to do this.

3. Contact a couple of local property managers to get an idea of the possible rental return. Here is a real-life example of why this is so important:

Example:

Joanne was looking at a property that was currently tenanted at $260 per week, and there were three months remaining on the lease. The asking price of the property was $300,000, and at that return it seemed as if the property, which had nicely satisfied all of the criteria, was going to be highly negative in cash flow.

We suggested that Joanne call a couple of other property managers in the same area for their feedback. Both of them told Joanne that $260 was well under the market value, and that they felt that a minimum of $330 could easily be achieved. This, of course, changed the figures dramatically and made the purchase a far more attractive option. By the time Joanne negotiated the price, signed contracts and then settled the purchase, there were only three weeks to go on the lease, and she promptly re-let the property at $335 a week (using one of the new managers, of course)!

Always clarify the rental returns by asking a number of different agents, as the difference that $30 or $40 a week can make might be significant.

4. If you have no personal debt, it might be useful to reduce your yearly costs in each subsequent year to reflect the reduced interest amount as you repay debt. Work out approximately how much per year you think you may be

able to pay off your debt. (For example, if you think you may achieve a $30 a week positive cash flow, then you should be able to pay $1,500 extra a year into the debt.) Be aware, though, that when calculating loan costs you only use the interest component of the debt, not the actual repayment, if that repayment is paying off Principal and Interest (P&I). This is because any part of the loan repayment which is not interest is buying you equity, and adding to your net worth, and this portion of the repayment is not tax deductible.

5. Try to calculate five years of estimated cash flows and ascertain if the property can remain or become positive cash flow during these early years. To do this you might need to inflate the rent by a small amount each year in line with what you can reasonably expect rental increments to be (usually at least inflation). Here is where vacancy rates can help (see Question Two). A downward trend in vacancy is a reliable indicator that rents may go up.

6. You may also like to consider some other possibilities and do some extra calculations to establish the impact. For example, what would happen if interest rates were to rise? Do a calculation with a higher rate and ask yourself if you could manage that eventuality. What would happen if you experienced four weeks' vacancy? Reduce the yearly rent by that amount and ascertain the impact. The purpose of this exercise is not for you to panic or change your mind about the property – it is for you to estimate what a negative event might do to you and decide if it is within your capacity to manage. Note that the Destinylive calculator has a comparison section which enables you to easily allow for vacancy and variations in interest rate, purchase price and other cash flow variables.

7. Where the cash flows you are getting are a little too negative for your liking, return to the calculator and work out how far the price would need to drop to bring the cash flows into a more comfortable range. It may be that a $25,000 discount off the asking price would make all the difference, and so this would be the target price you would aim to achieve. You may believe that people don't usually discount by that much, but I can assure you it certainly does happen. Be careful though – later in this book you will learn about how to establish market value. A listed price is not the suggested starting point for your negotiations, as that price is only what the agent has decided to try to achieve. You need to establish whether that price has any relationship to real market value. If you overpay for a property, any expected growth will take longer to achieve.

Example

A few years ago we were looking at a property with an advertised price tag of $365,000. I needed this property to be $330,000 to make it neutral for me, and so I offered $310,000 (which of course was laughed at). I didn't call the agent back, so after a few weeks he called me to see if I still had an interest in the property. We had a long conversation, during which he revealed to me that the vendors were committed elsewhere and were prepared to drop immediately to $350,000 if I was willing to meet them there. I told him that $320,000 was my top offer and away he went, to return with the news that the vendor simply would not go lower. I refused to move even though I had the capacity to pay more. Why? Because I needed to keep the power in the negotiations, and I had collected enough information to know that this property wasn't moving. Weeks passed again, and presumably the time period until the vendors had to proceed with their other purchase began to grow short. Once again, the agent phoned: this time to say that the vendors could go as low as $340,000. I stayed at $320,000 knowing that I must have been the only interested party, or he wouldn't keep calling me!

Some two months after my first offer we finally agreed on $325,000 – $40,000 below the asking price and more than a 10 per cent discount on what they had listed the property for. The key was that I didn't care about the transaction as much as they did, which gave me the position of power. I was also in control of the process, as I knew my figures and knew the market value.

Being familiar with exactly where you stand financially is crucial to avoid making emotional mistakes that will be expensive after you buy. Try to follow the above process with more than one property at a time, if you can find suitable properties that are available at the same time. This way, you will be a better negotiator, and from an emotional point of view, you will not be as disappointed if one of the transactions does not complete. Remember, don't undertake this process until *after* you have asked the 20 Questions – it is time-consuming and definitely premature before then to go into such detail, only to find that the property and area fail the tests provided by the other criteria.

SUMMARY

You are asking this question to be sure that you don't ask all of the 20 Questions and get right to the end, only to find that this area cannot deliver enough cash flow for you to afford to buy property there.

If you reach the end of this question and the results are that the cash flows require a large weekly input from you, then proceed no further. If, on the other hand, the cash flows are either within your capacity to afford (if negative) or positive from the outset then you should proceed to Question Two.

QUESTION TWO

What is the vacancy rate of the area?

You're excited because you think you have found the perfect property. It looks great in the picture and it would appear that you can get it for a good price. The financials all stack up and you are happy with the cash flows and the ability of the property to take care of itself from an expenses point of view. You'd live there if you could! Why not buy it straight away?

Let me tell you a story about Chris. Chris was 23 and dead keen on becoming involved in property investing. What he wanted was a property that would pay for itself. He could then plough all of his money into its debt, and after 10 years own it outright. The strategy was a good one for a young person who had no ties and big goals.

He went along to a property expo, an event at which developers promote their products, and was mesmerised by the fantastic models of upcoming developments, meticulously displaying the fine detail of each offer in three dimensions. These models even had little people, pools and cars on display. The developer to which Chris was attracted had spent tens of thousands of dollars building a full-sized section of one of the available apartments in the corner of his massive display, so that buyers could experience in real life what they were being asked to purchase off-the-plan.

Chris signed an expression of interest to buy a studio hotel room, after he was told that these apartments were selling like hotcakes and that even one day's hesitation could mean they would all be gone. He also took away all of the glossy brochures. Being a busy young guy, he carried out his research by reading the brochures from cover to cover, and did his calculations based on what the brochures divulged.

Using the forecast return and occupancy rates in this literature, Chris worked out that the cash flow would be a massive $100 positive, every week. That and the five-year rent guarantee offered by this developer were enough to seal the deal for Chris. He could not lose, he told me. Even if he had calculated incorrectly, he had lots of room to move, and anyway, there was a rent guarantee.

One year later it had all gone pear-shaped. The occupancy rate forecast at 80 per cent had materialised at a dismal 21 per cent – it wasn't even enough to meet the costs of the management company running the hotel. The rent guarantee, intended to be supported by the great cash flows from full occupancy, fell over. The value of his apartment on the market was 40 per cent below what he had paid, due to the fact that there was simply no second end use for a studio hotel apartment. Chris had no tenant, no income and no buyer. What he did have was a bank insisting that the debt still be repaid, and a sudden inability to leverage into more property due to his massive negative equity.

We can feel sorry for Chris, and then we can ensure that this never happens to us by carrying out our own research. Brochures from developers do not constitute viable research, and the information contained therein needs to be independently verified through many alternative sources.

After you have confirmed possible rental returns and clarified that the cash flows are valid, your next step is to assess the demand for the property from tenants. You may have clarified that a property letting at $300 a week can give you the cash flows you need, but if the demand is low and the property suffers periods of vacancy, your cash flows may be severely impacted.

ASK AN AGENT

Call a few local property managers and tell them you are going to buy a property and you are interested in their management services. Ask them how many properties they currently manage, and how many are presently vacant. If you ask a number of managers in the area this same question, you will get an instant snapshot of potential vacancy rates. For example, if they have 100 properties and 10 are vacant, vacancy rates may be as high as 10 per cent!

While you are speaking to them, ask for their opinion on current vacancy rates. Remember, they are not actually qualified to judge and, unless they have access to specific data, they will only be taking a guess. You are simply trying to gather as much information as you can, which you will then confirm against data from other sources. You wouldn't take the word of a property manager about vacancy rates if it was the only opinion you had, but in the context of receiving a lot of information about the same question from several sources, it may serve to confirm that vacancy rates are low.

One of the important things to do when you are becoming a property investor is to build a good team around you. If you find a property manager who is helpful to you at this phase of your research, and you end up buying in that area, then you should retain that same property manager to manage the property for you. Their willingness to give you information before you even become a client may well be a testament to how hard they will be willing to work for you once you do become a client.

USE REAL ESTATE INSTITUTE WEBSITES

Most countries have a real estate institute or association and some have many, with institutes in each state. Their purposes are many – from licensing and training of estate agents right through to the provision of data and lobbying governments for change. They all have websites and, while some are better than others, some of them may provide you with basic vacancy data.

These websites can be a mine of very useful information. While they all differ, the information you can obtain from these sites usually includes:

- information about each suburb's or area's average rental returns

- suburb snapshots

- market information

- guidelines for property purchasers, including information about the laws that cover both buyers and sellers

- newsworthy articles about property in general, and at times specific detail about relevant real estate topics

- information for landlords and tenants

- statistical data about property (although of course this is historical only).

The information you can collect from these websites can help you determine demand for tenancy in an area, even when they do not provide actual vacancy data itself.

USE OTHER WEBSITES

When in doubt, simply type a query into Google and you will almost certainly end up with information that is useful to you. There is definitely a technique to learning how to perform Google searches, however, and it takes some trial and error.

Once you have an area chosen, go to Google and type 'vacancy rates in [area]', then hit 'enter'. You'll get lots of data about houses and articles returned in your search, and it's time to scour them to try to get as much related information as possible. Make sure you validate the dates of any reports you find so that you can be sure that these reports are current.

THE IMPACT OF VACANCY

As an investor, you must establish the impact of any period of vacancy on your ultimate cash flow, so that you can determine if this is an impact you can bear. You might think that you can't manage even one week without rent – a week without, say, $300 may seem too big a price to pay. However, if you consider that a week without $300 equates to $5.70 a week for the year, and that you would also get an additional tax break for this extra loss, then perhaps it would not be as grave as you think.

Once you have discovered what the vacancy rates are in an area, you might wish to apply this percentage to your yearly rental return, instead of using the straight method of 50 weeks' a year rental return. So, for example, if your expected rental return is $300 a week ($15,600 a year) and the quoted vacancy rates are 3 per cent, you might like to do your calculations based on $15,132 per annum income ($15,600 – 3 per cent).

If your adjustment for an expected vacancy period will result in a further tax loss, you must make a related adjustment to the amount of tax you get back. Of course, the calculator at Destinylive will do this for you, but if you want to perform quick calculations on the spot, apply your rate of tax to the amount of income you are losing and this will give you the extra tax break. Then deduct this extra tax break from the amount of lost income to get a net loss.

Example

A 3 per cent vacancy on rent of $15,600 per year is $468.

$468 × 30 per cent (assumed tax rate) = $140

$468 − $140 = $328

$328 ÷ 52 = $6.30 per week

This is the extra weekly amount you would need to pay to cope with a 3 per cent vacancy rate.

At this point you can decide if that is a figure you can cover, or not.

VACANCY IN ONE-INDUSTRY AREAS OR SMALLER TOWNS

While it is important to work with current vacancy rates, you must check this particular data against information that you will be uncovering from future questions. I call this 'data syncing' and as we get through the questions I'll talk more about how you must sync the information you get from asking some of the questions against information you need to find with others.

It's critical to check any vacancy data you are able to uncover against information you will collect from other questions, like those about employment, demographics and incomes. When it comes to vacancy rates, in some areas, occupancy on rental properties can be sporadic. You need to work out why this is: is it due to the fact that the area exists for the purposes of servicing a particular industry? In these areas, when the economy is strong and demand for whatever service or product that industry provides is also strong, you'll see more people coming into the area for work and subsequently placing pressure on the available rentals. Rents will rise. Vacancy rates will be low. Values may rise too, if investors flood the area seeking properties with better than average returns.

In later questions we will examine just what is going on in terms of industry and employment in an area, so that you can determine whether or not a particular area is likely to have long-term, sustainable growth to the population and the economy, or shorter-term sporadic growth in response to the wellbeing of the main industry, or even the building of a significant piece of infrastructure which brings temporary renters to the area. Also be aware that for vacancy rates to be an effective measure, there needs to be enough renters in the market – an area with very low vacancy but also a low percentage of renters is not an accurate measure. Knowing these factors will then help you to better examine vacancy rates, to determine if they are a good indication of what might happen over the longer term.

TOURISM PROPERTY AND VACANCY

From time to time, you may come across an opportunity to buy a property that draws its occupancy from the tourism market. I am not a big fan of a purchase like this and in Question Eleven I will discuss the features, benefits and what I see as the considerable drawbacks of such property for the investor, and include information about risk.

At this stage, it's merely important to note that if you are considering buying such a property, it may be considerably harder for you to confirm occupancy levels. The brochures you are given by the property marketers will most certainly quote expected occupancy levels, but these rates are rarely based on reality.

The problems are:

- They will be based on the average occupancy rates of other tourism property in the area. Average rates take into account the best and worst performers and fail to compare like with like. You might be looking at an apartment in a three-and-a-half-star resort, while the expected occupancy levels are based on historical data that includes four-star and five-star resorts in the area.

- As these figures are based on historical data, they are not usually adjusted to take into account the impact of new developments on future vacancy rates. To continue the example above, it may be that there are many new resorts being built, but the number of people expected to visit the area is not forecast to increase. This would mean that existing developments would suffer, and rather than all of the resorts enjoying higher occupancy levels, all would experience a drop in levels because there would still be the same number of people seeking accommodation, but more options. Unless an area can show 100 per cent occupancy, with waiting lists, and there is data to show that accommodation is insufficient and extra accommodation is needed, the historical vacancy rates may be unreliable.

- Reported expected occupancy levels may have been formulated from data collected only in the peak times and may not have been seasonally adjusted.

- Reported rates may not take into account whether a particular event, which may or may not continue, was the catalyst for any recent high occupancy levels. For example, the Grand Prix period at the Gold Coast would attract full occupancy, and this period would then skew the overall result for the year. In addition, if the Grand Prix is subsequently moved from this area, it will impact on returns for investors.

• Tourism areas are notorious for coming into and going out of vogue. Historical occupancy data is an unreliable measurement of future demand.

It is difficult to establish a reliable indicator of future vacancy rates of property built for tourism. Checking with the local government authority about their expectations of future demand may help a little. Later, in the discussion about niche-market property (see Question Eleven), I will explain some safeguards for you if this is the type of property you are considering.

SUMMARY

You now have an idea of the cash flows of a number of areas on your list. You have also assessed the vacancy rates and have done some work towards confirming that the expected cash flows are possible on an ongoing basis. Vacancy rate points to demand – the higher the rate, the less the demand. If vacancy rates are tight, check that this is because of a genuine and lasting demand in the area and not just because there is a project which has brought temporary renters into the area. If the vacancy rate points to strong demand, then move onto the next question.

QUESTION THREE
What are the infrastructure plans for the future?

I recall a property which we bought in a less-favoured area of a capital city, about which many of the locals expressed surprise. Some were downright horrified!

I was in the area on the day the purchase was being finalised, quite by coincidence, as I was speaking at a function. I also had a radio interview, in which it was revealed that we had purchased property in the area, although the exact location was not divulged.

Later, during the event at which I was speaking, many people who had heard the radio interview approached me to discover where we had bought. As we were from outside of town (although I had lived there for many years prior), it was quite encouraging for many people that we should choose to buy in their city.

I still remember the looks on many faces as I revealed the name of the suburb in which we had bought. 'Don't you know about that area?', was the common query. Apparently, you did not choose to live in that suburb back in those days – you only lived there if you had no other viable option!

From my perspective, not only did the area satisfy the 20 Must Ask Questions®, it did so in spades! My research had uncovered the extension to the major freeway that would soon link this suburb more closely to the northern suburbs, the planned railway link, the new school, two new shopping centres and the imminent release of new land to cope with an expected influx of new residents. The fact that it was in the lower range in terms of its price, with a healthy rental return, indicated to me that there would be plenty of demand then and into the future. Since I wasn't going to live there myself, I didn't particularly care what other people thought of the area – I wasn't trying to keep up with the Joneses.

Four years later, it would seem that my instincts then were as accurate as they had ever been. There was a property price boom shortly after our purchase, which impacted on property values and saw the value of our property double. However, in an interesting twist, one of the suburbs that experienced the greatest degree of gain during that boom was – yes, you guessed it – where my property was! To make this purchase even better, we had deliberately bought a house on a larger block, and were immediately able to add a second dwelling, the value of which was double what we paid to have that dwelling built. It's been a great investment for us and it continues to do well.

This was not an accident. It was not an indication of the luck that my former radio co-host is still convinced I possess. It is, quite simply, a result anyone can achieve if they are willing to do the hard yards and carry out the research. When we bought that property, we knew that it would either be a great buy or a good buy. The things we discovered about infrastructure alone were almost enough to confirm a positive future for this area. The value of that property, which has tripled in the time we have held it, plus the value of the second dwelling which has also tripled, has provided us with substantial opportunity to leverage into more property.

Uncovering the infrastructure plans of an area is crucial. At the end of the 20 Questions, I will discuss growth drivers and the important role that infrastructure plays in determining potential growth (Chapter 6). For now, let's discuss what you should be looking for.

NEW DEVELOPMENT APPLICATIONS

While the supply of new housing is a demand and supply metric which I will look at later in this book, the degree of new development applications has particular relevance to infrastructure planning.

You see, in addition to having an exact idea of the population size, demographic mix and expected future population growth of their area, most local governments actually control it to some degree! So, if they are controlling the release of new land to an extent, but there are plenty of infrastructure plans coming up, it's more likely that there will be an improved demand for property in the area, and a lack of supply.

Local government controls development in a number of ways. Firstly, the release of new land for development is strictly controlled, not only to maximise its commercial value and to make money for the local government, but also to control the rate at which people move into the area. A sudden influx of residents into the area, possibly attracted by cheap housing prices and rental rates, can potentially create a huge problem for a local government unequipped to provide the basic services required.

Secondly, the rate at which new development applications are accepted, and the time it takes to approve them, provides more control over how quickly a population can grow. If a cap is kept on the amount of available housing, people cannot migrate to an area.

It's also important to consider development applications for commercial ventures as well. This is because in granting permission for new commercial ventures to be built, local government controls how valuable property can become. If major services are limited, a town or area will fail to thrive and the population will tend to stagnate. Allow major commercial ventures to thrive, on the other hand, and the people will come.

You are looking for either a significant degree of existing commercial development to be in place (in the form of shops and other service providers) or a good number of applications for these services to already be in the system.

THE PROVISION OF REQUIRED SERVICES

Population grows in two ways: through migration and through internal procreation. Either way, if a population is growing, the area in which people live must be able to continually provide for their needs, otherwise they will be forced to move away.

There must be adequate plans to provide schools, medical facilities and shopping centres if the population is growing. Public transport needs to be well developed. Where an area has limited employment opportunities, there must be adequate facilities in place to allow people to commute to other major centres to obtain work.

A great example of this is the Central Coast of New South Wales, Australia. Situated halfway between Sydney and Newcastle, it was once the domain of the retired and those Sydney residents who owned 'holiday shacks' to which they escaped regularly on the weekends. As property prices in Sydney moved beyond the reach of many, families began to look to the Central Coast for alternatives. Despite the limited employment opportunities available on the Coast itself, the excellent train network provides frequent services to Sydney every day: a journey that takes around 1.5 hours. Today, with a population hovering around the 400,000 mark, a staggering 60 per cent of the working population of the Central Coast make this commute daily. While employment still remains scarce, local government has met the other infrastructure needs through ample service provision, and housing prices remain reasonable in many parts of the area.

THE PLANNED UPGRADING OF INFRASTRUCTURE

Having suitable infrastructure in place or in the planning phase is one thing, but many areas outside of major capital cities suffer from poor-quality road systems, electricity and water supplies, and general area maintenance. If local government is addressing these issues, they are indicating their willingness to foster and encourage growth and change. If they consistently patch up or otherwise ignore these problems, the area may fail to thrive in the medium term and your investment will not grow as well as you had hoped. It is the lack of attention to maintenance of infrastructure which is usually the culprit for turning thriving towns into ghost towns.

SPECIFIC DETAILS ABOUT THE IMMEDIATE AREA IN WHICH YOU ARE LOOKING

Is there a plan for a football stadium to be built close to where you are finding good property? Are there plans to turn that vacant land down the road into a garbage tip? Is it possible that any of the land in that area will be rezoned as commercial or industrial? Is there a long-range aim for a nuclear reactor to be built in the region? All of these things and more will impact on future values. Before you get too deeply into asking the 20 Questions about an area, make sure, as far as you can, that no changes with far-reaching negative impacts will occur after you buy.

ASK THEM!

From your perspective, you want to know how progressive local government is and what their long-term and short-term plans are for the area. Ring them up and ask them! Have a conversation with the town planner.

Ask them:

- How do you see the population growing over the next 10 years?

- How long does it take you to approve a new development application?

- Are you approving applications for new shopping centres and schools?

- Are you allowing larger retailers into the area?

- Are you encouraging diverse commercial ventures?

- Have you committed funding to upgrade services and infrastructure?

- Do you have any major projects planned, or on your wishlist?

Ask if they have a publication that outlines their long-range and short-range plans. Many such documents exist, or at the least there are usually articles and papers published on local government and state government websites for you to download and view.

As a last task, type the name of the area into the Google search box and see what you get. You may find independent articles about events and plans for the area, forums, information websites and a whole host of other details. When it comes to infrastructure, no amount of information is too much.

FUNDED VERSUS UNFUNDED

Many local governments make a range of election promises which never come to fruition. In my time as a property investor, I have heard of many exciting pieces of proposed infrastructure which never materialised, and seen many property investors buy in areas where this promise of new infrastructure was made and not honoured, only to find themselves with property worth less than they paid, unable to dispose of it due to lack of demand.

There is a big difference between proposed infrastructure and funded infrastructure. Before moving ahead and buying a property in an area where a great new bridge, train station or freeway is said to be in the pipeline, make sure that the funds to create it are already in the bank.

SUMMARY

In order for people to remain living in the area, and for new people to move to the area, the infrastructure has to be either in place or in the pipeline. That infrastructure also needs to be funded, and not just on a wish list. Without suitable infrastructure, the population will begin to decline as people move away in search of the amenities they need. Infrastructure is one of the strongest growth drivers. If you have confirmed that there is plenty of the right kind of infrastructure, you can keep the area on your list and move to the next question.

QUESTION FOUR

What is the population, population growth and demographic mix?

When you're making the decision to buy property as an investment, you're likely to come across capital cities, outer suburban areas and even towns outside of cities which offer property at a good price. I have personally had success buying in some regional towns, even those which are some hours' drive from a major city.

However, the size of that area from a population point of view is a critical factor. When a town or area has 10,000 people or fewer, most people in that area tend to be related to someone else in some way. It is like one big family – the streets are named after the people who have probably lived in them for years, the pub or local bar is more like the local living room and everybody leaves their doors unlocked, because to steal from someone would most probably mean literally stealing from your family!

One of the things that I have discovered when examining these kinds of small towns or areas is that children who are born into these communities often feel a great need to flee when they come of age. For starters, in order to find a life partner, they most likely need to look outside of the area (since they are probably related to most people *in* the area). So they leave, find a mate and usually settle and raise their own families elsewhere. They are often motivated to move because work for the younger generation can be incredibly hard to obtain in some of these smaller towns. Education is often lacking too, and so many must move to get a good university education.

Because of this bleed of young people, the population in the area or town tends to stagnate and stay around the same for many years. This means that the local government doesn't need to provide too much in terms of infrastructure, and property prices tend to remain fairly stable.

When the population of a town or area reaches around 30,000 people, this situation tends to change. Suddenly there are too many people for everyone to have relatives everywhere, and the chances of finding a life mate within the area increases. Retailers and developers from outside of the area see an advantage to building, and there starts to be improvements. Young people become more likely to settle and raise their families in the area, and that increases the population even more. Infrastructure is built and there is more to do in the area.

This is the main reason why I suggest that you look for an area or town with a population of at least 30,000 people. Do note, though, that this doesn't apply to *suburbs* in larger *cities*. Where the 'area' you are searching is a suburb of an overall city, then while you still want it to satisfy the 20 Questions, it is okay for that suburb to have fewer than 30,000 people as the population has access to the infrastructure and economy of the whole city of which it is a part.

Many years ago, I was considering buying our first block of apartments. My Australia-wide search returned a town I had never heard of before (and whose name still escapes me to this day). In this town was a block of eight two-bedroom apartments, on the market for $340,000! The rental return was quoted at $100 a week for each apartment: a massive $800 a week rental return, or a yield of more than 12 per cent. Based on those figures it certainly would have been a great positive cash flow investment.

I asked many questions about the property and it seemed like a good buy. Then I asked what the population of the area was. 'Two hundred and forty-two,' came the reply. 'Thousand?' I asked. 'People,' was the answer! I quickly worked out that, if each apartment had four occupants (parents and two children), that would be 32 people. That would mean that 13 per cent of the entire population living in my apartments! I may have visions of grandeur, of becoming a great property baron, but I wasn't prepared to become *the* property baron of that town, which was also four hours from everything – the state border, the coast, the nearest supermarket.

POPULATION GROWTH

When you are eliminating areas from your list, questions about the *degree* of population growth are just as important as those about the actual number of people who live there. For example, I would prefer to buy in an area with, say, 30,000 people that has shown steady growth over the past few years, and has a local government committed to supporting and fuelling that growth, than I would in an area of 50,000 people where the population has stagnated or is in decline.

Try to ascertain, most likely from websites or bureaus which report population statistics, the number of permanent residents and the pattern of population growth over the past few years. If the population is growing, find out what is driving this growth, and establish whether these drivers are short-term or sustainable. This is another form of data syncing – seeing a growing population but asking the questions about what is making that happen.

Later in the book we will look at what makes growth sustainable, so that you can ask the right kinds of questions about the area in which you're looking.

DEMOGRAPHICS AND THE FAMILY

The most critical demographic group that you can have in an area is the family demographic.

Think about this for a moment. If you have school-aged children and have found an area where you like living, and there is a good school nearby, what are the chances you are going to want to move while your children are still at school?

Families tend to anchor to an area. They put their kids into school and then remain in that area at least until the last child has left school. This can extend to be between 12 and 20 years! During that time, the housing supply will more than likely start to dwindle. As other families want to join this stable community, they demand the smaller number of properties which are on the market, and that demand may well end up outstripping supply and place pressure on prices.

Of course, this is another question that must be synced against other data. Even families will move if the service provision is not there. Without schools, daycare, parks, sporting facilities and transport, after a while they will look to areas that have better capacity to service their needs, and the reverse might occur – an oversupply of property, a dwindling population and falling property values.

DEMOGRAPHIC MIX AND PROPERTY CHOICE

So, you have discovered that the area you're researching contains a high proportion of young families. As long as the population is growing, that's all you need to know, right? Wrong. To you as an investor, the most valuable information relates to the housing needs of the *type* of people who live in the area.

Let me tell you a story about an investor who I helped years ago. Some of you will remember this story from another of my books, but it is worth retelling.

Example

Ken, as I will call him, had decided to buy a property in Mount Isa, Queensland, Australia. In making this decision, he felt that he had asked all of the right questions and narrowed down Mount Isa as a viable choice.

Mount Isa is predominantly a mining town, although some believe that there is a burgeoning tourism industry. Regardless, the strongest rental demand comes from the miners who fly into town for the usual shift of 14 days and fly back home to their families for the break.

After choosing a set of three one-bedroom apartments that would have high appeal to the miners, who needed mostly a bed, a fridge and a TV, Ken had the contracts sent over to a local Mount Isa lawyer who had been recommended by the real estate agent. The lawyer's first call to Ken commenced with the comment, 'Clearly you're not a local. If you were, you would not be buying property in that part of town!'

Ken called us in a panic, asking if he should withdraw from the sale. I asked him to reflect on the type of tenant he had imagined living in his apartments when he chose them.

'Miners,' he told me.

'Do you think any lawyers might apply to lease an apartment from you?', I enquired.

'No!', Ken said.

'Do you think any lawyers would live next door to your apartments?', I continued.

'No!', Ken said.

'Do you believe that the demand from lawyers for rentals in Mount Isa justifies you looking for property that they would deem suitable to rent?', I asked.

'Of course not. They probably own their own homes,' he answered.

Ken was able to see that his choice was right, and that of course the lawyer was not going to approve. However, the lawyer wasn't going to live there, and nor was Ken. While he owned those apartments, Ken enjoyed not only full occupancy, but a suitable degree of capital growth too since the area had more than just the mining industry impacting the values of property in the area over the period that he owned them!

Almost every day an investor asks the question, 'Which is better, houses, apartments or villas?' I always reply that it depends entirely on who is going to be the tenant. There is no truth to the rumour that houses are better because they have land and land appreciates while buildings depreciate. Tell that to the many people who own apartments in McMahons Point in Sydney, which skyrocketed in value in the early 2000s, while houses in Concord, in the inner-western suburbs, hovered and dropped in value a little more each day. The value of the property you own is very much related to the demand for it from both tenants and buyers, and that demand will be dictated by the *type* of property they are seeking. It's a fact that in some areas apartments grow better than freestanding houses, and in others the reverse is the case.

At this phase of your research, you must look for information on who your target group will be in terms of tenants. Then you can choose the right kind of property for that group. If, for example, you determine that the population is ageing, then you should go for ground-floor apartments or low-set houses with little garden to maintain. Young families will need space and backyards. Professional couples will want modern apartments with lifts and security videos. Local government activity is also a good indication of what to expect – are they building senior-citizen centres, aged-care and respite-care facilities?

If so, they believe the population is ageing. Are they building schools, community centres and child health clinics? If so, families must be moving in. Is there a plan for a university or higher education facility? Yes? Then it looks like students and families with older children will be moving into the area.

In addition to finding information on the demographic mix of the area from local government websites and other sources, phone local property managers. You will already be asking them about vacancy rates, and it will be useful to also ask what types of property are in the most demand, or currently in short supply.

The decision to furnish a property, or not, like the choice of property type must come down to the ultimate use of the property. It is not universally true that including furniture increases rental return. In many areas, furniture is not wanted, as people look for properties into which they can move their own belongings. Conversely, residential houses and apartments owned in tourism areas, where people move for a working holiday, may well profit from the provision of furniture, and this furniture may be able to be added to your plant and equipment on-paper claims, depending upon the country in which you make your claims.

AGE AND ECONOMIC INFLUENCE

The other important factor that the demographics can point to is the potential for the economy to remain strong. In Question Seven I talk about the vibrancy of an economy. The demographic mix in an area will have a significant influence on the economy, and on the potential for an area to grow.

There are two main age groups which *may* present a future issue to you if you are not aware of them when you decide to buy.

The first group is young people aged 15–25. Where this group makes up a significant proportion of the population, you may face a situation of diminishing demand *if* other factors are not present. If you find an area that seems to have a significant proportion of young people, you must sync that data with data about employment (Question Seven) and Infrastructure (Question Three). Without suitable employment opportunities or appropriate services, these young people will likely move to other areas to satisfy these needs, and the population will begin to shrink.

The second age group which can present a problem is the ageing demographic. Where an area has a large, ageing population, the economy will be soft, even where there is adequate infrastructure and appropriate service provision. This is because the retired population has less money to spend in the area, and there is usually less business being conducted within the area. There is often a higher turnover of property in an ageing area, both through natural attrition (death) and residents moving into aged-care or retirement communities. This means that the supply of property usually meets or exceeds demand. All of these factors mean that price pressure is simply not there, and we often see property prices in ageing communities remaining soft for many years.

PROPORTION OF HOMEOWNERS

Most countries have a Bureau of Statistics website which provides an abundance of census data. Among the statistics you can obtain is the number of households under homeownership. This can give you a snapshot into the rental market – is it substantial, or is it very small? Some real estate search engines or other property sites also provide such information on an area, and you may wish to review the relevant data in your country.

This is where it is important to understand exactly what you are looking for. Some may think that a higher proportion of renters is better, but this is not actually true. Areas with a high proportion of renters to homeowners usually have more itinerant or less affluent populations. As you will see in later questions, these features of the population can impact on the capacity of property values to grow.

You are aiming for there to be enough homeowners that the area has secure, long-term residents who contribute to the local economy and stay in their homes, reducing supply as the population grows and the demand increases. In such an area, as it becomes more in demand because it satisfies many of these 20 Questions, pressure comes to bear on existing property, especially if that area also has little in the way of new land available. Prices go up because people want to stay there, and they don't sell.

You also need enough renters to make your purchase of a property to rent out worthwhile. If there are too few renters, then there will be less demand for your property, and you'll need to decrease your rent in order to attract a tenant from a small pool. Even if values do go up you may not be able to afford to keep holding that property if you cannot get enough income to support the expenses.

A good rule of thumb is to have 30 per cent of the population renting and 70 per cent owning either outright, or with a mortgage. Most statistics websites will provide this kind of detail.

All of this information will help you with the next question, which relates to the competition in the area.

Confirming that the population is of a number and demographic mix that will ensure long-term demand for what you eventually buy is an important part of the puzzle. If an area or property does not meet these basic guidelines, delete it from your list.

SUMMARY

Population is an important growth driver. Not only does population need to be growing consistently, but it needs to be made up of the right kind of demographics.

Families will be the strongest demographic driver of all demographic groups. Where there is an abundance of families in an area, and this fact is met with suitable infrastructure and amenities, the area should grow into the future. If the area you are looking at has a strong family demographic, move onto the next question.

QUESTION FIVE

What are the supply/demand metrics of the area?

At this stage, you have been able to confirm that the area in which you are looking has the potential for positive cash flow property, or for property with cash flows that are acceptable to you, that shows every sign of being able to be enhanced in the very near future. You have also confirmed that the population can support ongoing demand for tenancy, and you have a good idea of what kind of property to buy, as you have explored the demographic make-up of the area.

Now you need to know a little more about the supply and demand metrics of the area. This helps you to establish three things:

1. Whether you are going to be able to find, and keep, a tenant.

2. Whether there will be a sustainable demand for your property while you hold it, so that it not only grows in value, creating equity for you, but it has a high degree of saleability if and when you decide to sell it.

3. Whether you are too late for that particular market or, in some cases, too early.

It may seem perfectly reasonable to conclude that, since the area is mostly populated by families seeking to rent housing with at least three bedrooms, your purchase of such a property will result in sustained tenancy. However, what if a developer has plans to build a new subdivision that will adequately cater for the demand from that target group? It will have an immediate impact on your ability to attract and retain tenants and also an impact on the supply of housing, which affects the value.

ESTABLISHING POTENTIAL SUPPLY/DEMAND

While it will be impossible to establish all the plans for the future, there are some things you can do to find out whether the area will see active development in years to come, or otherwise. Here are some pointers.

Supply of new housing

In your discussions with the town planner, ask them if they can tell you more about development applications. If you can discover the number of development applications that are currently lodged, it will provide two things – a potential (but vague) indication of the number of people who may be taken out of the tenant pool, and an idea of how much new property will flood the market. Remember, you have already discovered information about the current state of affairs (that is, how many households own their residence and how many rent) in your demographics search. You are only working with estimates, and this is by no means an exact science, but at least you can get some idea of any pending impact on your ability to attract tenants and have a property that will grow. Some time ago there was a relatively new suburb in Melbourne which was being heavily developed. Spruikers were doing a good job of moving these newly developed properties onto investors, who bought them based on the figures provided to them about the current rent return and the most recent growth trends.

What these investors didn't consider was the fact that firstly, with mostly investors buying the new dwellings, there was about to be a major influx of supply and secondly, that the population of that area was growing only at the same rate as all the other suburbs around it.

The bottom line was that rents fell dramatically once all of these new dwellings were sold, as the rental market was suddenly flooded with available rentals. The other thing which happened was that there was an oversupply of three-bedroom two-bathroom houses (which was the most popular style of house being built) with no corresponding spike in population growth. It was many years before these properties even returned to a value equal to what had been paid for them, and while the investors waited for that to happen, their rental returns were far lower than they had hoped.

Land availability

Ask about land availability and new land releases. You want to know about both land that the local government plans to release and any submissions for subdivision by private owners or developers that are pending. This is particularly important if you are looking in areas with a high proportion of rural land. Regular land releases keep the prices of existing housing down, so while they may not necessarily affect your ability to obtain a tenant, they may impact on the growth potential of property in the area.

Stock on market

It's important to find out how much stock is presently available in a particular market. This one is a little tricky, since the question 'How much is too much?' begs to be asked. Obviously, if 50 per cent of all stock in a particular market is listed for sale, you would need to ask the question 'Why?'. Is it because of a large new development or is it because everyone is fleeing the area due to some underlying cause? If the percentage of stock on the market seems to be high, then you need to data sync this fact with other data that you obtain from asking other questions.

On the other hand, if the percentage of stock on the market is very low, for example below 5 per cent, this doesn't automatically mean that it's a great place to buy. The last slowdown in Sydney, for example, led to severely reduced listing as no-one wanted to sell their property in a declining market, and equally, no-one wanted to buy them! In this case the low level of stock indicated a declining market, whereas in other areas this low level of stock may indicate that demand is outstripping supply.

You should be able to get an idea from the main real estate sales websites in your country as to whether there is an abundance of available listings or not. Once you have this data, check it against the other questions so that you can establish the reasons behind the level of stock on the market at that time.

Days on market

Days on market is an indication of the number of days the average property in the area where you are looking sits on the market before it sells. Many real estate search engines or websites, such as www.realestate.com.au/invest (for Australia), provide detailed information relevant to investors, or you can do a Google search and find this information. The figure itself doesn't always mean much, although if the average property is sitting on the market for, say, 150 days that's a pretty clear indicator that the demand is low. Conversely, an average time of, say, 20 days is an indicator that the market is hot, providing there is sufficient stock on the market.

In either case though, you must again sync the data with other data. A high number of days on the market in an area that satisfies all of the 20 Questions could simply mean that you are well ahead of the crowd. In those circumstances, though, you must accept that it could take some time for the market to begin to heat up, and in the meantime, you will experience low or no growth. You must go back to what you have discovered about your own immediate needs – cash flow or growth – to then decide what to do.

Remembering that all investors should be aiming for cash flow and growth, initially one will be more important to you than the other. If you have low personal cash flow now, then the higher the cash flow the better and you may be able to wait for growth. Under those circumstances, waiting for growth if the rents are good won't be a problem for you. If you have high cash flow but little equity, then you may be able to stand a lower cash flow for now but you need growth soon. Those high days on market in an area satisfying all 20 criteria may be a warning sign for you to find a different area. You'll find a complete discussion of this important cash flow/growth analysis, and how to work out what is right for you, in my book *How to Achieve Property Success*.

Online search interest

Checking out how many people are looking at each listing on the real estate search engines is a good way to get a quick snapshot of the present demand in the market. It's an immediate figure and lets you know straight away how much competition you face.

You can usually find this figure on most real estate search engines, or do a simple Google search and you'll find it. It is most often displayed alongside the average number of people for an entire state. You might be looking at Whittington in Victoria, Australia, for example. At the time of writing there were 1,573 people looking at every listing, compared to 909 in the state of Victoria. This is clearly a hot market and one that you have likely missed. In addition to paying top dollar for any property you find, your capacity to negotiate will be virtually nil, since you'll have plenty of competition.

Go and search in Point Cook, Victoria, and you'll find 242 people (at the time of writing) looking at each listing, compared to that same state average of 909 people. It is a low-demand market, but why? Use the other questions to work out if you've missed it, or if it might be an up-and-coming market that you can beat the crowd to buy into.

Again, I can't express strongly enough how important this data syncing is. A low-demand market can mean many things, just as can a high-demand market. The figure you uncover here is a very small piece of the puzzle you are putting together.

Zoning and town plans

Enquire about the zoning of land in the area by contacting the local government authority. Where a strong rural protection order exists, it is less likely that larger properties will be subdivided for new building. Where subdivision of larger plots is allowed and encouraged, your new property may suffer from low growth until the land begins to become scarcer.

You also need to know about potential commercial zoning in the area. Imagine if you bought a property in a quiet street, only to find that commercial or 'mixed use' zoning applied to part of the street, and a shopping strip was built there at a later date. This may impact negatively on your property and make the area less desirable.

On the other hand, sometimes a change of zoning can be beneficial. It may be that all properties in the area you're looking are presently zoned for single dwellings, but a plan exists to alter the town plan to allow medium-density dwellings to be built. This may then open an opportunity for you to develop a property by subdividing or adding a second dwelling at some time in the future. Properties where the zoning changes like this can become more valuable even when the market is stagnant, as they become targets for small developers.

Be careful though, as the reverse can happen. You might purchase a property because it is zoned for medium-density development, only to find at a later date that the town plan changes and only allows single dwellings. If you paid over the market value because you thought you could later develop the property, you could end up the loser.

Be sure to check the town plan in regard to zoning and be certain there is not a draft town plan in the making which changes any zoning you may be relying upon.

Discounting

The next important metric is known as vendor discounting. This is the average percentage that properties in the area are being discounted before a property is sold. The higher the figure, the lower the demand. The closer to zero that figure, the closer to listed price properties are selling for, and the higher the demand.

I'm sure you know what I'm going to say next – sync this data to other data. Areas with extremely low discounting are obviously in high demand, and I am never comfortable buying in high-demand areas, no matter how good the prognosis. This is because in those high-demand areas I *know* I will pay top dollar, and with buying costs I am already behind the eight ball. Prices have most likely already gone up and I am coming in at the closing stages of that market's growth. While properties might still rise in value, it is unlikely that they will go up too much more once this vendor discounting figure is close to zero.

On the other hand, a high-vendor discounting figure doesn't mean the opposite. You might have uncovered an area with great potential, but others just haven't worked it out yet. Keeping in mind that initial growth could be slow if you are first into an area, it can be a good way to stockpile future growth assets as long as you don't need the growth to do that stockpiling through leverage.

Auction clearance rates

In some states and countries, auctions are an accepted and prevalent way to sell property, while in others they are a rarer method. If you are buying in a state where auctions are preferred, then the auction clearance rate becomes an important demand metric. When auction clearance rates slip below 60 per cent the market is considered to be softening. When they head above 80 per cent it is considered to be hot. Somewhere in between is usually an indicator of a healthy market.

TOURISM

If buying into a hotel or serviced apartment complex interests you (see Question Eleven for more details about niche-market property), you have probably been introduced to the project by an advertisement, brochure or someone working on a stand at a property show or expo. The information provided to you may seem detailed but is most likely skewed by the developer's enthusiasm to sell their project – and therefore it may not be reliable.

The main problem you face when purchasing in such a development is one of oversupply. Take the Gold Coast area in Queensland, Australia, as an excellent example. While there is no doubt that tourism is strong and healthy throughout the Gold Coast, it is also a fact that new holiday accommodation continues to be built in abundance. Take a tour around any last-minute accommodation website and you will see the literally dozens (even hundreds) of offers for incredibly low-priced accommodation, as operators compete for a finite tourism dollar. With building showing no signs of slowing, and the local government seemingly approving new applications from developers with no hint of a slowdown, the situation will tighten in the future.

Previously, I discussed the need to clarify whether the forecast occupancy figures provided in marketing material are based not only on future demand, but also on future supply. The developer of the property you are interested in may truly believe that they are responding to a clear demand, but so might 20 other developers! Without a corresponding expected future increase in demand, you could end up with your new property on a last-minute website, desperate to find an occupant.

Be sure to quiz the marketers on this point. Ask them to prove to you that consideration has been given to *future* demand. If they tell you that demand is increasing, ask them to show you the evidence. Why is it increasing? What is happening in the area that will attract more visitors? Is there a campaign by the tourist bureau to increase marketing, provide more activities or attract the overseas market? Asking such questions will help you to avoid ending up like Chris in Question Two, owning a white elephant that you cannot unload.

To obtain further information about tourism, type 'tourist information centre [area]' into your Google search engine. Each state and area has its own tourist bureau or tourist information centre, and many smaller towns and areas have tourist information on their local government website.

OTHER SPECIAL PURPOSE PROPERTY

In some areas, local government is actively seeking to cater for a known demographic group by fast-tracking applications for property that satisfies specific needs.

Consider the market for accommodation for the aged. When people retire, often they move to warmer climes. Studies have shown that the number of Australians, for example, who will be retiring after 2020 with either no family home (as they have rented all their lives) or with all of their wealth tied up in their family home, has been vastly underestimated. Many in this latter group of people will be seeking to sell their home to realise their cash; both groups will need rental accommodation in their twilight years.

Because of this, many parts of South East Queensland have been targeted as suitable areas to build accommodation appropriate for this age group. It could be that you have identified an area you believe has many good qualities, which also has a large population of retired people, and therefore you are considering an apartment purpose-built for seniors.

Similarly, university towns have greater needs for student accommodation, and so developers have made provision for this demand by building apartment complexes to cater for the specific needs of students.

If these are target groups that you believe may suit you, or suit the area in which you are buying, ensure that you take extra care to consider how well this market is catered for. Universities can only have a finite number of students at any one time, and rampant development of student accommodation in these areas will result in oversupply.

Equally, the seniors' market is large but not unlimited, and once retiring baby boomers are no longer demanding such property, the secondary market may fall off. This demographic is also likely to be proportionally less in future generations. People will also retire later and later as governments change the rules around retirement income streams. These are critical factors to consider as they affect the long-term performance of your property – and the long term is when you are likely to need it to perform the best. It's great to have your property in demand and yielding a good return when you first buy it, but you are likely to be working during that time and deriving income from employment. Later, when you retire, and you require the property income to support you, the last thing you need is for demand for what you have bought to reduce, as your income will be impacted.

SUMMARY

Supply/demand metrics can help you to establish where in the market cycle an area sits. An area doesn't have to be presently under strong demand to be a potentially good area to buy in, but it must show the signs that demand is increasing. This question helps you to establish what is driving demand and how likely that demand is to continue. You are now ready to proceed onto the next question.

QUESTION SIX
What are the trends?

I've already mentioned earlier in the book that historical information is not much use to you, and that it is information about the future you really want to know. If you think I am now doing a backflip by including this question – don't worry. I said that, but what I didn't say is that the best thing about historical information is that it can tell you where *not* to buy!

Share investors use a number of methods to determine how they are going to buy and subsequently trade their shares. One of these methods, known as technical analysis, requires the investor to plot share movements on a graph in an effort to predict trends. Investors using this method believe that a pattern does emerge over time that repeats itself, and so it is basically a matter of tracking the pattern and looking for the bottom of the cycle to decide what and when to buy. Wouldn't it be wonderful if we could do the same thing with property? It would make everything so much simpler – we wouldn't even need the 20 Questions, as the graph would tell us where to buy and when.

While many 'experts' still cling to the old 'property cycle' theory and advise that it is all as easy as buying at the bottom of this cycle, much has occurred over the last 20 years to make picking the bottom of the cycle harder. In the days before the internet, when mums and dads raised families, worked and by and large didn't become investors, the property world was much less complicated, and tended to track the economy more closely. If they did invest in property, they bought it around the corner, and so the impact of supply and demand was kept local and much easier to forecast.

Now we tend to have hundreds of property cycles all over the country, all behaving differently from each other. Some of these cycles are, curiously, not even linked to the economy – we could be in economic slowdown at the same time that property values in some obscure town are rampantly galloping upward. Much of this has come about because accessibility to property has increased through the use of the internet.

Share investors also use a method known as fundamental analysis. Just as it sounds, this technique involves looking at an individual company's intrinsic characteristics (its fundamentals) to establish whether it is likely to make a success of its venture. Investors who rely on this technique believe that a share price is ultimately linked to the ability of the company to meet its financial and other goals. And in many ways, this is what we, as property investors, are doing by asking the 20 Must Ask Questions® – we are establishing whether an area has the right characteristics to increase in value in the long term.

Thus, there is a place in our research for considering past trends, as these may be able to give us some valuable information about the future. Knowing what *has* happened may help us to determine what *will*, or *will not*, happen in the future.

GROWTH TRENDS

I did an interview a few years ago in which I was asked to discuss what makes an area grow. I talked about all of the intrinsic growth drivers that an area must display (which are discussed in Chapter Six) and also about the 'flow-on' effect that property increases in adjacent regions may have on an area.

As an example, I quoted the incredible price increase that Bunbury, south of Perth, Australia, had enjoyed the previous year. On average, property prices had increased by 36 per cent, and while this had sent yields plummeting (since rental returns had yet to move), existing property owners would reap many benefits from this increase.

'I had better get off the phone and run off and buy in Bunbury, then,' was the response of the journalist. 'No!', I said, 'It's too late.' While values in Bunbury did indeed continue to increase for another year, for anyone needing to achieve a positive cash flow it was too late to buy. However, Bunbury still had much to teach us that we could take away and use somewhere else. You see, there must have been an abundance of reasons why Bunbury experienced this sudden and unprecedented growth. We simply had to find out what those reasons were, and then find another area that looked like Bunbury but had not had its boom yet!

So, if you are hearing about great growth in an area, here's what you should do:

- **Research the area and ask Question One** – what is the cash flow? You may not have missed out just yet if the cash flows are still positive, or just beginning to be negative. If they are very negative, chances are that the growth is nearing an end and, if you buy there now, you will be on the tail end of a boom. You could wait a long time for the next growth spurt, and you would be supporting a negative cash flow while you do so.

- **Find out what is driving growth.** Later in this book I am going to devote an entire chapter (Six) to the differences between intrinsic and extrinsic growth drivers. Extrinsic growth drivers bring short-term, unsustainable growth, while intrinsic drivers deliver the opposite – sustainable growth. If extrinsic growth drivers are presently in play, it may be a false reading and so may not be a worthwhile area in which to buy. Researching this will help you to work out whether it is growth that is due to influences which may not be lasting, or not.

- **Find out the growth figures for the past few years.** If they have been good every year, the area may be headed for a slowdown, *unless* you have discovered other things that may continue to fuel the growth, such as new road or rail links. Look at any area that has had a sudden boom in price. How long does it last? The longest period I have seen was just under three years, and even then, those people who bought property in the final year of that growth saw the values topple by the amount of the previous year's growth. So, in reality, that area only had two years of growth from intrinsic factors, then a year of frenzy-fuelled rises which were subsequently not sustained.

- **Compare the growth of the past few years.** When was it greatest? Is the growth increasing each year, is it staying even, or has the past year seen less growth than the year before that? This will show you a trend.

If the area in which you are looking has had low growth for many years but has a lot of growth drivers or has similar characteristics to another area that recently grew very well, it may be an area to watch. For example, previously I mentioned Bunbury. After I heard about the great growth that was happening, I would have looked around for another area that was a little like Bunbury. I would have looked for similar population levels, similar proximity to a major centre, and demographics that mirrored those in Bunbury.

Past growth trends can tell us if an area is still growing and is still affordable in terms of cash flow, or whether we have truly missed the boat. They can also give us valuable knowledge to use when seeking an alternative area. History always has so much to teach us, if we only look and listen!

RENT TRENDS

Rent trends are harder to establish and harder to read, but since you are in the process of collecting a lot of information, it will be useful to add details about how rents have progressed in recent times. Be aware, however, that interest-rate increases or decreases alone will have an impact on rental returns all over the country. When interest rates rise, most landlords look to recover their additional costs by increasing the rent. When they fall, landlords can offer discounts in those areas where vacancies are rising, because they have less outgo to cover.

In countries where the average lease period on most properties is six to twelve months, it can take up to that period of time for a rent movement made in response to an interest-rate change to filter down. In countries where typical rent periods are longer, then it can take even more time than that. So, when you are looking at how much rents have risen or fallen over the past few years in any area, first of all make sure that these increases have not happened within six to twelve months of an interest-rate movement, and check to see if similar movements have occurred in other areas.

Rents are affected by many different factors, and these factors can result in increased demand for rentals. Just as with growth drivers, an increase in rents has to be examined in terms of the reasons for the increase. It could be a large infrastructure project, such as a major road upgrade, bringing workers to the area to complete the project. This would create a sudden, but short-term, pressure on rents and landlords could start charging more. Investors might see this increase in rents and buy property in the area, which then impacts on values too. Once that project is completed, and the workers move onto the next project or become unemployed, demand ceases and rents fall. When you examine rental trends, be sure to also examine the underlying influences of those trends to establish the reasons for the increase or decrease, and whether that factor is sustainable.

Some real estate search engines, real estate institutes and foundations, and private data companies have information about historical rent trends. Usually, you can just type in a year and a suburb or town and see the median rent at that time for that area. Other data which exists includes median rent return, but always be careful when basing any of your decisions on median figures. They take into account the high and the low rent returns in an entire area, and where an area has both high-end and low-end properties, this won't be a useful indicator. It could be that the high-end properties are experiencing higher vacancy and therefore lower rent return and the lower end properties have had no change, and yet the overall figure will show a fall.

———

What are we trying to read from analysing the two trends? If both growth and rents have increased really well over the past three to five years, you may be too late and the cash flows will be very negative. So, choosing property in an area such as this would be done in the knowledge that you will be supporting the property until you can repay some debt and reduce your costs.

If neither growth nor rental returns have moved much, and you have confirmed population growth and infrastructure planning, then both are more likely than not to increase in the future. Values growth is most likely to occur before yield growth. If the cash flows are negative, this will probably change fairly quickly.

If rental returns have increased without values growth, find out why. It may be due to the nature of the employment in the area, and in Question Seven we will examine this more closely. You must confirm that factors to drive growth are present, otherwise you will buy a property with positive cash flow that does not grow. One such property in your portfolio may be acceptable, as it is nice to have the cash flow; however, if all of your properties are like this you will find it difficult to leverage into more property, since you need growth to do that.

If growth has occurred and rental returns have not increased, and the cash flows are not so negative as to be out of your capacity to cover, ask the rest of the questions quickly, because you may have uncovered a great area!

You can get some basic growth data and recent sales results and suburb profiles from almost all real estate search engines. Once you have this, use your trends analysis to get a feel for what has happened, what is happening and what is likely to happen. Keep in mind, however, that this is only one question: as with all of the 20 Questions, it is the combination of answers that should guide you, not the answers to a sole question.

DATA SYNCING

This particular question needs two types of data syncing. You must explore the other 20 Questions to work out the reason why rents are rising or falling or why values are rising or falling. You need to eliminate the possibility that the area is coming out of its growth cycle and heading into the downturn, or that it is influence from factors outside of the area which is causing the growth in values or rents.

You also need to use these trends to consider your personal circumstances. If rents are going to be affected, and you are an investor with low personal cash flow, then how will you manage if you have to decrease your rent to attract a tenant?

If growth is going to slow down, or even go backward, how will this affect your capacity to leverage into more property? If you are an investor with little equity or savings, you need growth to occur as soon as possible in order to be able to build your portfolio.

SUMMARY

Examining the trends assists you to do two things: firstly, to work out whether rents and values are rising or falling and, secondly, to establish if you are too late to be buying in an area. If an area which has satisfied all of the questions up to here has a plateauing growth or rental trend it might be because you are too late – prices and rents may already be too expensive and causing demand to drop off. If, however, the area has vacancy trending down, rents trending up and growth trending up, if it satisfies all of the other questions so far *and* those trends are relatively new, then you may have found an area that is pre-hotspot. Keep going!

QUESTION SEVEN

Is there economic vibrancy in this area?

The next thing you need to know about an area is whether its own micro-economy is vibrant. It's possible that an area can exist in a state or city that is in economic downturn yet be an area where the micro-economy is going well. This is why just knowing how a country, state or city is performing from an economic perspective isn't enough.

Economic vibrancy is crucial in order for an area to experience *sustainable* growth. Being economically vibrant attracts spending into an area and keeps the population growing. Areas that plod along with zero population growth, eventually dying off to become little more than ghost towns, are usually those that also lack economic vibrancy.

Economic vibrancy is measured by the economic indicators of an area: basically, little pieces of information that, when put together, tell us more about a larger system. While you will not be trying to produce an educational dissertation about economic vibrancy in any of the areas you are examining, there are some things you can discover that, collectively, indicate whether an area or town is economically vibrant.

THE SUCCESS OF BUSINESS IN THE AREA

An area where business is not carried on is an area where everyone works *out* of the area and commutes to their job. It's possible that these people may be living away from their jobs for lifestyle reasons, but in the main, areas where there is little in the way of business – both large and small – contain people who are far more likely to be itinerant. If they meet new friends or a life partner, or find a new job out of the area, they may move away, as they have no roots.

Where you are considering buying in outer suburbs of a capital city, it's less likely that the people in that suburb will work nearby, and as long as transport isn't a problem (meaning there are buses, trains and a good road network) then that suburb's success will be dependent on the success of the city to which it is attached. However, if the area you're researching either has no access to public transport or is more of a regional or an out-of-town suburb, then the area itself needs to be economically vibrant. The further an area is from a capital city, the less it can be influenced by the economics of the city.

Note that I am not saying that an area *has* to be in a capital city in order to provide a good outcome for your investment, nor am I saying that areas outside of capital cities cannot perform equally to those within a large city. What I *am* saying is that any areas not able to benefit from a large city's economy must have a thriving economy of their own.

Once residents begin to open businesses in the area, it becomes more secure. If you live and work in the same area, you are more likely to spend your money there, and so the cycle commences and the economy becomes more vibrant.

Look for:

- local business associations that have strong membership, such as chambers of commerce

- low vacancy on commercial premises – where there is a high rate of vacancy on commercial premises, business may not be thriving

- applications in local government for new industrial, retail and office developments – the people who build these will usually do a fair amount of research first to ensure they will be able to sell them

- the provision of the basic needs of the community through local business – service stations, mechanics, hardware stores, supermarkets, community centres, department stores, and so on.

A Google search should uncover the details of local chambers of commerce and other business associations as well as give you an idea of the vacancy on commercial premises. Local government can outline for you plans for commercial or business park developments.

THE AVERAGE TIME A RESIDENT STAYS IN THE AREA

Further questions in this book will help you to understand more about why people live in an area in the first place. This is an important thing to know because it helps you to establish whether the population is itinerant or stable.

When we bought our very first property, the marketing agent told us that 10,000 people a year moved into the area, and he was right. He didn't tell us that 12,000 moved out, because it was a holiday area and most of the people living in that area were on working holidays, with jobs in hospitality. For many years we had tenancy issues! Thankfully, we worked out early on that the nature of that area was that most people lived there for the short to medium term; once we furnished the property, we attracted more tenants. Had this transient population been due to other reasons, and resulted in a diminishing population, it might have been a serious problem. Of course, that property never really grew much in value, and the only reason we ever really hung onto it was because we eventually saw a pretty good cash flow. The property didn't hold us back from further investing because we had plenty of equity in other properties we bought around the same time. It was a good lesson in how important knowing about resident stability really is!

Look for areas where the average time people remain residents is around five years, as this provides stability. Local government should have this type of information available.

INNOVATION

Imagine you decided to start a business. You come up with a good idea and, initially, the business does well because everyone wants what you're offering. Then, as the years progress, more and more people begin to copy your idea, and there is more choice available in the marketplace. Even if you still have exactly the same product as you had when you began, the number of people who use your product will begin to diminish as the demand is spread across the many more options which have become available.

The way that you can claw back market share is to innovate: either come up with a better idea or make the idea you had better than it was. You'll need an edge over the competition, if you want to get back to where you were before you had competitors. You'll need to have something which is *better* than the competition.

The same principle applies when it comes to areas that may be the most in demand from residents. In an effort to sustain and promote economic vibrancy, and continue to attract people to the area, some local governments adopt an innovative approach to their responsibilities. While the ability to spend money depends very much on how much money a local government has and the grants it can secure, innovative planning can always take place. A desire to attract interest in the area through the erection of public facilities and attractions, the maintenance of public areas and the provision of appropriate services to the community when they need them, are all signs of an innovative and progressive local government. Such an area will also experience economic vibrancy, as people generally like to be part of such a forward-moving community.

Once you have checked out the website of the local government (which in itself may demonstrate innovation), talk to them and see what their feelings are about innovation. Find out what their plans are for the future. See if they are matching their planned service provision to the needs of the demographic which we have already identified as being the one most likely to drive growth – that is, families. If the local authority has a significant plan to provide amenities and the lifestyle that the family demographic desire, and a clear vision for the future of the area, then it is also likely to support population growth, which then flows on to create property price growth.

HOMEOWNERSHIP

Earlier I talked about the percentage of homeowners to renters, and this statistic also impacts on economic vibrancy. Since you are possibly going to become a landlord in this area, you will want to be able to confirm a healthy demand for rental accommodation. There are many areas which provide a wonderful lifestyle for residents, but on closer examination of those areas almost everyone who lives there is a homeowner.

A good degree of homeownership is important in an area because, generally speaking, people who own their homes have a vested interest in keeping the asset in good order. However, in areas where everyone owns their own home, there will be a lack of tenants. On the contrary, in areas where everyone rents, the population is less stable, the economy is less vibrant and the long-term capacity for growth will often be affected.

The ideal situation is where there is a balance between the two, with homeownership being slightly higher than the number of rentals. Economic vibrancy is the result of this sound balance between available rental accommodation and homeownership.

EMPLOYMENT

Employment is one of the biggest drivers of property price growth, alongside population growth. Where a population initially grows but subsequently struggles to find employment, the trend of population growth will reverse as people move away looking for work. Not only is it critical for you to know the percentage of people unemployed in the area, and how this compares to the national average, but you also need to know how this is changing between census periods.

Basic census data is available in most countries, and this data can be very valuable for you. Depending upon how often a census is undertaken, you can usually obtain data from at least the last three. If you look on your country's census bureau's website, you will be able to obtain data for the area in which you are interested. You will be able to view a lot of good information and make a comparison across several time periods. In Australia, the website is www.abs.gov.au and the census section you need is QuickStats.

You want to see firstly that unemployment levels are tracking the national figures at least or, better still, are lower. Typically, employment levels at around 6 per cent indicate a reasonably strong economy. Employment levels around 4 per cent indicate an exceptional economy. Once employment figures dip below 4 per cent the area reaches what is known as 'full employment'. The reason that full employment is not measured at 0 per cent is because there will always be a percentage of the population who choose not to work, and during any one measurement period there will be people who are in-between jobs, but declare their status as 'unemployed'.

When an area is in 'full employment', it may also experience 'underemployment'. This is where part-time workers cannot find jobs suitable to their skill level. The issue for an area in this situation is that those people unable to find suitable jobs for their skill level may subsequently leave the area in search of appropriate work. So, while full employment is a desirable influence for the growth of an area, underemployment is one that *may* result in a higher turnover of tenants.

Employment data will be divided into age groups and this is important to you when choosing a property *type*. High youth unemployment, where the employment figures in their parents' age bracket are strong, might be okay but it means you have to be sure that you choose a property suitable for the parents, not for the younger generation. If the young people are unemployed they're probably living at home, and so houses will need to be bigger to accommodate them. This is a great example of that data syncing – what one piece of information tells you can become an important consideration in another way altogether.

If high unemployment exists in the older age brackets, and that figure is making the overall figure look bad, it might be that employment in the other age groups is still at a good level. Under these circumstances, that ageing population who cannot get work might be the result of very low employment in the younger brackets – the younger age groups may have all the jobs. You can see how this could mean that the area is going to do well in the future as the older generation moves on. If, on the other hand, there is high unemployment in those older age groups and most of the population is aged, then the area is one that you'd best stay away from. Areas with ageing populations generally take a very long time to turn around, if they do at all, and change demographics to those of younger age groups. They also have much softer economies as retired people spend far less in their communities.

High unemployment across all categories is an alarm bell, particularly if there seems to be no real reason for it. Under those circumstances there must be an indication of low economic vibrancy, such as few businesses in the area, or lack of transport to take people to jobs elsewhere.

The second thing that becomes important is the trend for unemployment. Is the figure getting lower or higher over the various census periods? If it is still a little high, but there is a decided downward trend, find out why. It could be that the area is becoming more economically vibrant, but you are just a little ahead of time. Again, you would need to measure these results against your own personal needs for cash flow and growth to work out if you have the capacity to speculate on what may be a great future hotspot.

MEDIAN HOUSEHOLD INCOME

Median household income, and the change it goes through over a number of census periods, is a great way that you can work out whether an area is becoming more affluent or not. Some wonderful investing can occur if you find what is essentially an 'ugly duckling' area and invest in it before it becomes a beautiful 'swan'.

Now, while not all ugly duckling areas undergo this change, some certainly do. I'm sure at some time or another you've heard a property investor bemoaning the fact that they could have bought in an area years ago, when no-one was interested and the prices were cheap, and now that area is the latest trendy hotspot. Perhaps you've said it yourself!

Areas become trendy when the lower socio-economic element start to move elsewhere, and those people interested in renovating and caring for houses as owner-occupiers move in. It often happens in those areas that have some good qualities, like access to transport and proximity to services, but have been previously largely held by government housing agencies.

Examining the median household income, and what is happening to it over various measurement periods, can give you an idea of the improving affluence of an area. Where the median household income is increasing faster than the national average, you may well have found an area that has a changing demographic and a different kind of resident.

It's not necessary for a positive change in median household income to occur between census periods in order for you to find an area economically attractive. However, a negative change may well be a sign of other underlying issues that may impact on economic vibrancy, and a positive change can be, as I said, a great sign of improving affluence.

Census data generally reports median individual income, median household income and median family income; just ensure that when you compare these figures across two census periods you include some weighting for inflation. For example, I would expect that the figures reported for 2016 will have naturally inflated by 4 per cent per year since 2011. A higher increase than that may indicate greater economic vibrancy, lower than that may indicate decreasing economic vibrancy.

Here I will remind you again that this question represents only 5 per cent of the total information you are trying to collect about an area. Don't let a negative answer cause you to abandon that area as a lost cause – find out if there are other explanations. However, if, at this stage, the areas you have been looking at haven't been stacking up under most of these questions, eliminate them from your list or put them aside for further review in another six months or so.

SUMMARY

Economic vibrancy underscores an area's ability to continue to grow over time and withstand short-term falls in demand. An area needs commerce, jobs and a good flow of income in order to keep its own micro-economy strong. Where an area is part of a city, it can benefit from that city's overall strength, but where an area is regional or in a smaller town, it must have these characteristics within the area. If you have found an economically vibrant area you can move onto the next question.

QUESTION EIGHT

Is this an area likely to experience the ripple effect?

Some years ago, my good friend Peter Switzer interviewed me for Q business radio, the Qantas inflight radio channel that airs various business and expert interviews. As usual, his interview was comprehensive and well done, and as Peter has an interest in property, he had asked appropriate questions.

In this interview I talked extensively about the success I had achieved by investing away from the considered hotspots and into areas that I had examined and decided were potential *future* hotspots, with some of these areas being regional towns which were, I felt, being overlooked.

Shortly after I had done the first of two interviews, the founder of a large 'club' for investors (and I use the term 'club' very loosely) circulated his regular newsletter, in which he claimed to have heard this interview on a recent flight. He claimed that I was advising people to buy cheap property in far-flung areas with little hope of any positive future. In short, he had managed to take what I had said and twisted it to support the fact that he himself was selling property in capital cities (at what I believed were inflated prices) to his club members.

A short time later, I was at a property show and speaking on the topic of growth drivers. I overheard a 'property investment expert', attempting to sell his overpriced property to one of my readers, commenting to her that it sounded like she had been listening to 'that Margaret Lomas', the way she was speaking about buying property with no hope! If I didn't already know that both these people make their considerable profits from the sale of expensive property that sometimes has highly negative cash flow, I may have taken offence.

The point that I am trying to highlight by relating these stories is that the strategy I teach does not necessarily involve 'cheap' property, nor does it include 'far-flung areas'. All properties, in all areas and in price ranges that you have established you can afford, should be considered until the process of elimination provided by these 20 Questions indicates they should no longer stay on your list.

If the properties being spruiked by the individuals who choose to speak out against my strategies stack up under the scrutiny of the 20 Questions, by all means go ahead and buy them. That is unlikely, however, since the properties they sell are generally confined to specific areas, and by now you know that areas become ripe for investing for a short period only. Unless these people have access to property everywhere or keep changing the areas in which they develop property, they are unlikely to continually be able to offer you property that satisfies all the criteria, all of the time.

Just as important as all of that is the relationship between these cheaper areas that I may appear to favour and the ones which are more expensive. This question relates to that relationship.

From the questions so far, you can see that we are looking for cities, suburbs or towns that are either major centres or cities in their own right, or are very close to, or part of, a larger economic region. Being able to access the services they need, when they need them, is crucial for the residents of any area. In the previous question we looked at how services within an area bring economic stability, as they keep money within the micro-economy, which in turn provides jobs that allow people to buy housing and pay rent in an area, so that they remain and consume goods locally. In addition, being able to access all the things they need, such as groceries, car servicing, sporting facilities, schools and even entertainment (movie theatres and so on), will ensure that people will stay in an area. People who have to drive far from home to fill up with petrol or drop their kids to school will soon tire of it, and more than likely move away. This is why people who live and work on tropical islands tend to stay for such a short time – the things they need on a daily basis are just too hard to come by!

IS IT ALWAYS NECESSARY TO BUY IN AREAS CLOSE TO A CITY?

No, it isn't. In some parts of every country, there may be smaller towns or areas of 4,000 to 5,000 people situated within a 20 minute or so drive from a major centre of more than 50,000 people. In this situation, when people can access the services they need and find employment by taking a short drive to the bigger town or city, you might be able to keep the area on your list and keep working through the rest of the questions. However, if that small town is three hours from the nearest petrol station, delete it for now.

Do be aware, however, that the window of opportunity in these smaller areas is sometimes short-lived, even though it can be a good one. While it happens that such smaller areas can grow really well, they more often present short-term opportunities to buy, ride the short wave of growth and then sell again. They could be growing simply because that nearby bigger area has become too expensive, and once the smaller area has grown a little and is no longer considered as much of a cheaper alternative, the growth may stall.

If, though, the close major centre keeps growing and growing, as some do, the smaller area may eventually be the recipient of 'ripple effect' growth that continues to occur.

THE RIPPLE EFFECT

By this stage, some of you will have decided that the ability to get a positive cash flow (or close to it) immediately or within the near future is more important to you than achieving better than average growth. This doesn't mean that you have decided that you don't want growth at all; simply that you want or need to maintain a certain standard of living today and cannot afford to contribute too much cash to your property investing strategy. So, in order to be able to start a property portfolio now, you may have eliminated highly negative cash flow areas from your list, which means that many parts of some capital cities will have been eliminated.

You may still have some suburbs in some capital cities on that list, however. There are many parts of major cities that are not only exceptionally affordable, but have either a positive, neutral or very small negative cash flow once depreciation claims (if available) are made. In addition, as prices begin to plateau in many cities where good growth has just occurred, the rents begin to move again. We then see a return to better cash flow in some previously high negative cash flow areas. So, don't eliminate capital cities out of hand simply because you *think* you won't be able to get good cash flows – do the research that will confirm or contradict this idea.

When a large centre or capital city experiences a sudden and possibly unprecedented increase in its values, people who wish to buy homes suddenly find themselves priced out of the market. If a homeowner already has a slice of the market, upgrading is easier, as they will be moving about in the same market. However, where a homebuyer is looking for their first home, where an apartment owner wishes to move into a house, or where a person is transferred for their job from another area, they will often find that they cannot afford to buy.

Instead, they may look outside of the immediate area, in the hope that they can find something for a more reasonable price. People can and do commute upwards of an hour each way, each day, to work, and consider that the savings they make buying into a cheaper market are well worth the costs associated with this commute.

This means that areas close to a recently booming major centre, or suburbs adjacent to more expensive and popular suburbs, will most likely benefit from the 'wave' or 'flow-on' effect within a year or two of the boom. Your job as an investor is to find the areas where the most recent major growth activity has occurred, draw a circle at a one-hour commuting distance from that major area, and look there for property. Then, ask the 20 Must Ask Questions®!

Many, many years ago, after the 1980s boom had come to Sydney and then slowed down, property on the Central Coast (a one-and-a-half-hour drive from Sydney) and in Wollongong (45 minutes away) was available at exceptionally good prices. Less than $100,000 easily bought a substantial property within walking distance of a beach, with many properties available for well under $50,000.

Within 10 years this situation had changed considerably: as the population in these areas swelled massively, prices rose and rose and rose. For a very long time these areas saw consistent growth, year in, year out, until finally the cheapest available housing became close to par with less expensive housing in outer Sydney. These two areas essentially *became* outer Sydney!

LOOK FOR LOW CITY VACANCIES

When the combined effect of a recent price boom and low vacancy rates for rentals in any area occurs, renters are forced to widen their search for suitable properties to rent. During a rental shortage some areas can report 20 to 30 applicants for each available property, meaning that the unsuccessful applicants must look elsewhere. Some innovative property managers have even tried holding rental 'auctions', leasing the property to the highest bidder! If an area is showing this type of full occupancy, with waiting lists, and property is now considered a little too expensive for the average buyer, then it is likely that demand for rental in adjacent, previously low-demand areas will increase. The ripple effect will occur for rentals, meaning that the values of houses in adjacent areas will also grow in response to improved demand.

EMPLOYMENT, THE ECONOMY AND THE RIPPLE EFFECT

Data syncing becomes another important task when considering whether the ripple effect will, in fact, boost demand from renters and buyers and subsequently cause an area to grow.

Where the adjacent area is easily accessible, via public transport or suitable road infrastructure, from the popular area where full occupancy is causing ripples, it is likely that the ripple effect will occur. Residents can, and will, relatively easily adjust to an increased commuting time for employment if it means they can save money on either a purchase or on rent.

Where that adjacent area has its own vibrant economy, and plenty of jobs, then residents may also accept moving to the area and changing their employer in order to improve their lifestyle and their financial situation.

However, in an area which is near a booming area but has no suitable transport infrastructure linking it to that area, or no employment available within the area itself, the ripple effect is far less likely to occur *unless* the local government can show a strong future plan for those things to come to the area. Data syncing is critical when it comes to determining whether the ripple effect can apply.

SUMMARY

The ripple effect doesn't necessarily always affect property. However, if you have found an area which is adjacent to an area with all of the required features, which offers similar kinds of properties but at much lower prices, and the neighbouring area has become too expensive, there is a good chance that the area you have found will benefit from the ripple effect.

Your list should be starting to get a little lighter and easier to manage by now. Let's move on to Question Nine.

QUESTION NINE

Is there diversity of industry in the area?

A few years ago, my husband and I were ready to buy another property. I think it may have been property number 30 or so, and I wanted to thoroughly retest the accuracy and validity of the 20 Must Ask Questions®.

I began the search as everyone should – not knowing exactly where I was going to buy and (as I live in Australia) using Australia as my starting point. As I moved through the questions, areas began to drop off my list until I was left with a small list of about six. In the final analysis, only two remained.

I had found a block of four apartments in each of these areas, both at around the $500,000 mark. So, I began my search into the reasons why people lived in the area.

In one of the areas, where the population was nearing 60,000, I discovered that they export from this area hundreds of millions of dollars a year of sustainable, clean and green horticultural produce, including dried fruits, olives, grains, vegetables, citrus, grapes and wines. Significant health and education services in the area provide employment for medical and teaching professionals, and being on the border of three states, local tourism is an industry in itself. Mineral sands mining was becoming another significant industry; 15 per cent of the population work in retail. There was an expected boost to tourism and employment in the hospitality industry, and unemployment figures were falling.

Researching the second area uncovered the fact that the 30,000 people living there work predominantly in the mining industry, with retail and service work following. Beef cattle was also farmed there but did not make up a significant proportion of the jobs.

Our decision to buy in the first area was made because we felt that the industry was diverse enough to support people wishing to cross over from their chosen trade or occupation. If something were to fail in one area of produce (such as the grapes, for example), then the people previously employed in that segment had plenty of other options for work and would not have to move out of town. The diversity of industry also provided a sense of stability to the area that was attractive to us as investors. Once we added to that the innovation shown by the local government in tendering for lucrative government contracts such as a solar tower project, we felt secure about our choice.

While the second area was certainly thriving, I didn't want to be in a position where I became alarmed at movement within the mining industry. I remembered the closing of BHP in Newcastle and the angst it caused and didn't want to have to go through that. Given that a significant number of residents would be miners – probably the majority of my targeted tenants – I felt I would be too exposed to this market.

Since that time, the mining town property has performed miserably while the property we eventually bought (and sold five years later) gave us a fabulous cash flow while we held it and a $125,000 profit when we sold it. Our decision to sell was to free up the equity to buy in another area where we believed a newer and better opportunity existed, but during our hold period the property did well.

Any area which is based on a single industry is highly risky, and the miserable results of too many mining towns is a testament to that. Be sure that the area in which you are buying has many diverse employment opportunities, and only buy in mining towns if you have money to lose.

CONFIRM THE INDUSTRY

If everyone in the area works in just one or two major industries, you are at high risk of ending up with a property that struggles to even get a tenant in the event that the industry fails. Worse, its value might fall and if you are forced to sell, you could find yourself under severe financial duress.

When I wrote the first edition of this book we were in the middle of a mining boom, and mining town properties looked like a fabulous investment. I warned readers to be careful, stating that the boom couldn't last. I was right, and too many people paid top dollar for properties that subsequently fell in value by up to 80 per cent. Many people bought more than one property and there were many bankruptcies as a result.

Another important point to consider is whether the other industries in town exist simply to support the major one. For example, in a mining town, the hospitality, retail, education and health industries may seem to employ a reasonable number of workers, but without all of the miners, these industries would probably not need to exist at all.

You must confirm what people do for a job in the area by going to the Bureau of Statistics and examining the employment information again. Find out the categories of work that people are involved in and be sure there is a good spread across many categories. Then, visit the local government website and any tourism websites to further confirm that there is diversity of industry, and that the majority of people do not work in just one or two industries.

CONFIRM THE FUTURE HEALTH OF THE MAJOR EMPLOYERS

This is where things get a little harder, but by no means impossible. This step requires some data syncing, and also some guesswork.

In many areas where you may consider a purchase, the local industry may not be a deciding factor at all. This is because it may be a suburb of a city or larger regional area, and the unemployment figures are low, meaning that there are plenty of job opportunities across all industries. The failure of one large employer or industry may not be reflected in falling property prices because people can remain in the area and obtain another job.

In other areas though, where large companies employ a significant proportion of the population, the failure of one company may have a bigger impact than you would hope. While there may be plenty of other large employers in that area, those employers may not have jobs available, and so those people who lose their jobs may have no choice but to move to another area. This of course floods the market with properties both for sale and for rent.

Another influencing factor is often market sentiment. The announcement of the closure of a major employer in an area could have an immediate impact on property prices if the *perception* of homebuyers is impacted. Here are two good examples with different outcomes.

Elizabeth is a blue-collar suburb of Adelaide, Australia. It is also an area with a significantly high proportion of unemployed people, particularly young people. The announcement that the major employer, the Holden car manufacturing plant, was to close had an immediate impact on property prices, and they fell significantly. It was an interesting effect, since the suburb is part of a capital city with strong employment, and the local government had committed to retraining to assist with any displaced employees.

A few years later, over in Corio, Victoria, the Ford plant also announced its planned closure. Corio is further from Melbourne than Elizabeth is from Adelaide, and yet the results were different. Subsequent to the announcement, there was a short period when prices stabilised (that is, didn't grow) and then, as the closure got closer and materialised, a sudden boom in prices.

What was the difference? Well, many things. Corio is adjacent to what was, at the time, a booming Geelong, a regional area with good transport links back to Melbourne which offered a great lifestyle, affordable property and plenty of service provision. Elizabeth also had good service provision, but nearby areas weren't faring that well in terms of property growth. While both had a high proportion of social security recipients, Elizabeth also had high youth unemployment and a crime problem. There was, I believe, also the fact that Melbourne people are accepting of the fact that they may need to commute an hour each way for a job, whereas the smaller city of Adelaide provides most people with job opportunities that are within 20 minutes of where they live.

It's likely that the ripple effect saved Corio, and its price boom was quite significant. Elizabeth will recover, as people realise that the closure of the car manufacturing plant isn't going to spell the end of employment opportunity, but it is going to take a while and a more significant change in demographics for this to happen.

When you're considering what people do in an area, what makes them buy property there and why they stay, think about those major employers and what their main business is. Is it something which is at risk of being made redundant by advances in technology? Do they manufacture a product which may have decreasing demand? What proportion of the population does each company employ? What other work is available for people to do (either within the area or within a relatively easy commute)? There may be many diverse employment opportunities, but if a bulk of them lies within one company, there will always be that risk that the company will close and property will suffer as a result.

SUMMARY

Confirming diversity of industry in the area where you are looking is a hedge against unemployment. Where there is only one major industry or employer, the risk to you becomes much higher. Be sure to confirm not only that are there many industries offering employment in the area, but that these industries are independent of each other and do not need each other to prosper and survive. If you are satisfied that your areas of interest meet these criteria, you are ready to move on to the next question.

QUESTION TEN

What is the live-ability of the area?

Throughout this book I've talked about remaining unemotional and going about this entire process from an arm's length point of view. You are not going to live in this property, and chances are your personal feelings about the area won't be a good measure of its investing potential.

Whenever I buy a new property, I make a point *not* to go and look at the area or the property itself. Why? Because I know that, by nature, I am a very 'touchy feely' kind of person. I cry at weddings and babies. I laugh easily at silly things. I am driven by emotions, and that very thing which makes me sensitive can also be my biggest enemy.

One of my best investments so far has been in two duplexes I purchased in a most unfavourable suburb in Adelaide. Before purchasing, I did all of the research and asked each of the 20 Questions. The area satisfied all the criteria and I proceeded to purchase these properties 'sight unseen'. That isn't to say that I didn't get lots of photos. I even had a local property manager visit to reassure me that the properties were rentable.

The properties doubled in value in the first four years. After that they sat pretty stagnant for a time. However, by that stage my rental return was 10 per cent so I was happy. After 10 years in this market, I made the decision to subdivide and develop. I turned the four properties (two lots of two duplexes) into eight three-bedroom villas. In doing so, I didn't add anything to my equity due to the fact that I borrowed to effect the development. Nevertheless I *did* quadruple my cash flows, since the rent on each of the new villas was double that on each of the old duplexes. In addition, because Australia allows depreciation write-offs, my tax position improved incredibly as I had eight brand new villas to write off.

I have visited the area since that first purchase – in fact, I did so shortly after buying. When I did so, I remember my alarm at what I found there; I was immediately uneasy about the purchase. Had I made that visit prior to buying, I am absolutely positive that I would not have gone ahead with the purchase. The area does not have what I personally seek in an area where I'd want to live, and I most certainly would have rejected it on instinct.

You can see how skewed that instinct would have been. Now, when I visit the area, I see many examples of redevelopment just like the ones I have just completed. Other people have also seen the benefits and now the area is changing dramatically. I expect future growth to continue to occur as the demographics keep changing.

Having said all that, even though you don't have to buy in an area that you would choose to live in and reject those where you wouldn't live, there are some basic things about the live-ability of an area that must be present for it to have any chance of taking off in the future.

TRANSPORT

I have referred in earlier questions to the importance of people being able to commute to work from where they live. Access to suitable transport options is also important for more than just the workers. Without suitable public transport to get people to any services available in the area, these services mean nothing. There needs to be an extensive bus, train or light rail network which extends to link up any major services. These services include schools, sporting facilities, shopping precincts, parks, childcare centres and community centres.

Without suitable transport, everyone will be expected to have a car, and probably more than one if the area also has a lot of families. In areas where people have two cars, we tend to see a more affluent population and property values which are high, with low rent returns. Typically, they won't be areas which make a profitable investment because they are already past the stage of being a hotspot and are now considered blue chip!

AMENITIES

An area has a significant amount of live-ability when everything you need is within walking or easy commuting distance. Considering that we are looking for areas where families can anchor and then raise their families, what are the most important amenities? I'd say education, health care, sport, shopping and entertainment! If all of these things are not catered for in an area, the live-ability score will go down considerably. Take care not to consider things which aren't important as being a good growth driver. Things like gyms, movie theatres, cultural centres and bars are all nice to have, but don't necessarily cater for the demographic which can have the most influence on property price growth.

WALK SCORE®

The Walk Score® identifies how close everything is to the bulk of the population and whether or not they can walk to most amenities. It has its place in your research, but be careful not to give it too much significance. These days, driving or using public transport, as long as it is only for short distances, is more than acceptable and with many areas being quite large in geographical size, not everyone can live within walking distance to everything.

It is useful, though, to consider it when you are data syncing. If there are not a lot of amenities and the Walk Score® is really low, then this could be a negative factor for the area.

AFFLUENCE SCORE

The affluence score relates back to family income. The lower the family income and the more social security recipients in the area, the lower this score will be, rated out of 10.

The closer to 10 the figure is, the more likelihood that it is an area you have missed, or which is well out of a suitable price range. Such an area is likely to also have a low rent return and a low percentage of renters.

The closer to 1 this figure is, the less likely this area is to become a hotspot any time soon. It's an area that probably has a high number of renters and a significant population receiving welfare.

I like this score to be not only around 5, but also for the area to be situated adjacent to an area with an affluence score above, say, 7. This is because affluence usually spreads as the more affluent suburbs move out of the price range of the average buyer, and the ripple effect often means that the area with the lower affluence score starts to see a different demographic moving in, keen to be close to that affluent area.

CRIME AND SAFETY

While an area's demographics do change from time to time, and crime statistics can also change over time, safety is an important factor for both homeowners and renters. An area with a high crime rate (usually associated with a high unemployment rate) will only become more appealing for prospective residents when this rate reduces. In the meantime, not only might you struggle to obtain a tenant, and find growth rates impacted as the demand from future buyers may be smaller, the tenants you attract when you own a rental property in such an area may be less desirable. This can end up being a costly exercise.

You can usually find information about crime rates from a simple Google search. One word of warning, though: a high crime rate doesn't always mean an area fails to thrive. There are plenty of examples of areas that were formerly considered unsafe which had a significant change in demographics and became good investments, particularly for those who took a leap of faith and invested before the crime statistics began to reduce. Such areas were usually surrounded by better areas, and so benefitted from the ripple effect that we examined in Question Eight. So be sure to consider this possible eventuality in any area that you are looking at.

HIP SCORE

It is useful to mention the hip score, but only insofar as it might add a very small amount of attractiveness to an area that you have already decided meets all the criteria.

In a nutshell, the hip score represents how trendy an area is. It relates to the availability of elements that adults look for, like bars and restaurants. It's an especially useful score if you are considering buying in an area that will target young couples, but may be not so important if you are targeting families.

In an area where the hip score is really high, I like to look to the adjacent areas where the score is not so high. Just as the affluence score can mean that a ripple effect is likely to occur, the hip score can have a similar effect on areas adjoining those which are the most 'hip'.

WHERE TO FIND LIVE-ABILITY INFORMATION

A Google search can reveal a lot about an area's live-ability. You can also find a good breadth of data at www.microburbs.com.au if you are in Australia. I find this the best place to source a lot of the above information quickly. You could also ask trusted property managers about these aspects of live-ability of an area.

SUMMARY

Live-ability is not about whether you personally like an area. It is about the ability of the area to deliver the kind of lifestyle that the demographics of the area are looking for. Some of the factors of live-ability can also become part of the ripple effect – for example, as neighbouring areas become overpriced, people will move into adjacent suburbs to benefit from the live-ability of the overpriced area.

— *Chapter Five* —
HALFWAY THERE!

YOU ARE NOW halfway to having a finite list of areas in which you would definitely consider buying. You'll notice that most of the questions so far have related more to the overall area and the target demographic of the property that you may subsequently buy.

Once you are at this stage, you are likely to have narrowed down your search of areas to a couple of particular areas which have satisfied the criteria so far. You will most definitely have eliminated many areas that you may have started looking at, because they didn't stack up when the questions were asked. Apart from looking at a few properties early in the process to work out cash flows, at this point you shouldn't have your heart set on a particular property, because you have only been narrowing down *where* to buy, not *what* to buy. If you began this process because you had seen a property that you liked, and wanted to work backwards to work out whether it was situated in an area that satisfied sound investing criteria, then by now you should know whether to go further with your research for that property, or whether to ditch it altogether. If you do, then all is not lost – at least you probably now have a list of alternate areas that do suit.

Now is the time to get a little more personal and property-specific and begin to examine what you are looking for from a property perspective. The next questions will ensure that what you buy ends up being the right kind of property, and a sound investment. Read on to Question Eleven!

QUESTION ELEVEN

What is the principal purpose for this property's existence?

You are more than likely at the stage of your research where you have found an area that seems like it may make a prudent investment. You've done most of the detailed, hard work, and eliminated areas that just won't be suitable no matter how good a bargain you can get.

It may be that the areas that you have remaining on your list simply offer an opportunity to buy a standard residential house or apartment. If this is the case, this particular question will have less relevance to you.

On the other hand, your research may have led you to an area where it may be prudent to invest in a property other than a standard residential house or flat. The term 'niche market' is applied to this type of property – this means that the property has been designed for a purpose other than standard residential leasing.

I've never been a big fan of buying niche-market property, and this is most likely because I have seen too many of them not perform as forecast by the seller or as hoped by the buyer. Because of the very nature of niche-market property, the risk when you invest in such a property is amplified by the fact that you have narrowed down your potential market of both renters and future buyers. If there is an economic impact which affects that market specifically, then even a well-bought property may fail to deliver the expected results.

However, if it looks as though a niche-market property may be something that you wish to consider, be sure to check your risk profile in Question Twelve before proceeding any further.

When you researched the demographics of the area, you may have discovered that it is frequented most by holiday-makers, or that it seems to have an abundance of retirees or students. That being the case, you may wish to explore the opportunities available in forms of property other than standard residential. Here are some of the alternatives.

TOURISM PROPERTY

A tourism property is simply a property that you buy for the purposes of letting to holiday-makers and travellers. There are several different types, as discussed below.

Holiday houses

A holiday house (or apartment) is any residential property that you choose to let for short-term accommodation. It may not be let on a holiday basis when you look at it, but it may have a lot of features that lend itself to this market: it may be near a beach or located close to a popular holiday spot.

A property such as this most often looks like a standard residential property. It will usually be self-contained, with a number of bedrooms, a kitchen and bathroom. In most countries that provide tax advantages for property investors, the tax treatment is the same or similar to that of residential property. In some countries higher tax benefits apply, such as a shorter period to write off any depreciable items, given the shorter-term nature of the tenancy and the recognition that depreciable items may wear out more quickly. It's useful to check with your own tax department if these added tax advantages apply, since they can be useful to assist with cash flow in those early years.

Property such as this is usually managed by an ordinary property manager, who may charge an additional fee to cover the extra activities they must undertake, such as more consistent marketing, more regular letting, and arranging constant cleaning and maintenance. Alternatively, you could retain a specialist holiday property manager. These days, many people use websites such as Airbnb or Vrbo.com to list and self-manage a property like this.

We have a house at the beach. It is very old and has been converted into two flats. It rents out for exorbitant rates, but only during the summer and Easter holidays. In our case, we have also seen some good capital gain in this property, although this wasn't an expectation when we purchased it – it was originally a pure cash flow exercise which paid off. A purchase such as this can work, providing you are sure that the minimum rent you can expect to receive during the short time it is rented is enough to produce a reasonable cash flow for you, and you can manage this cash flow over the entire year.

Holiday apartments

A holiday apartment will usually exist in a block of apartments (or villas) with an on-site manager who lets the apartments to holiday-makers. The manager is retained by the body corporate to both take care of and let the property; they may or may not own one of the apartments but will generally at least live in one in order to be on-site 24/7. In some circumstances, this caretaker may be one of the owners of the property who has taken on these additional duties for a fee. Their agreement may include rights to use common property (such as a reception area) in order to operate the letting service. This common property is still owned by the owners of all of the apartments in the complex.

Unlike a hotel, these apartments are fully self-contained and do not usually come with a daily cleaning option, although some managers elect to offer this as an added service, which is paid for by the apartment owner and covered by the rent received from short-term tenants. Where it isn't included, the responsibility of arranging and paying for cleaning at the end of each occupancy period (or sometimes on a weekly basis) falls to the on-site manager or the owner. Rent collected on an apartment like this is given directly to each owner after costs are deducted.

Holiday apartments are most often strata titled or some form of community title, and the only difference from an ordinary shared title apartment is that the on-site manager lets the apartment out for you. Also, they will keep a close eye on day-to-day maintenance, so you don't have to employ a property manager. You must, of course, pay for this service separately from the body corporate fees.

It may be acceptable to buy a holiday apartment if you have a realistic opinion of its potential net income. For example, if 30 per cent occupancy is enough to deliver an even cash flow, with anything more than that extra, buying an apartment in an area with low occupancy may still be a viable option. If, on the other hand, you need at least 80 per cent occupancy just to break even, then such a purchase needs careful consideration. When looking at such a property, make sure you find out the net return after all costs – this is rarely quoted.

Hotels, resorts, serviced apartments and managed apartments

There are various names given to this type of property, but basically this category covers all property where the property investor owns the title but has almost nothing to do with any ongoing operation of the business which occurs within that property. These types of properties fall into a separate category because their management is normally different. Question Seventeen will take an in-depth look at their property management arrangements and explain the 'management rights' or 'professional management agreement' arrangements that are often in place on them.

Many investors are attracted to these types of properties because, in the marketing material, it appears the return is much better than standard residential. This might be true, but there are often much higher expenses also involved, and so the bottom-line returns may actually end up being worse.

In most cases, buying a property such as this involves relinquishing most of your responsibilities to the manager. As the manager usually owns equity under these arrangements, it is most likely that they will be calling the shots and your voice will not really be heard. There have been a lot of problems in the past in relation to the failure of these ventures, so double your due diligence and be very sure that you can stand the risk that this type of investment brings.

OTHER NICHE-MARKET PROPERTY

Seniors' accommodation

With the population ageing all around the world, the emergence of property specifically designed for the over-55s has become a booming industry. While it can take many forms, typically seniors' accommodation will consist of a small one- or two-bedroom apartment with a courtyard, in a community complex. These days there is more and more luxury seniors' accommodation being built which still retains the features of higher-end, more spacious property but has access to the facilities sought out by seniors.

Depending on the individual complex, there is usually available a range of services that people normally seek in retirement – a bowling green, possibly a pool and gym, and a community hall. It may or may not also offer the option of providing regular meals, property cleaning and laundry services.

Some such properties are simply standard strata titled or community-titled apartments that are marketed to senior tenants over the age of 55 – they are not aged-care facilities as such, and do not provide care for the aged on-site. Others do have aged-care facilities and assisted-living arrangements.

In some cases, these apartments can be very small and are designed for the specific needs of seniors. This can make them unattractive to the general market, which means that demand for a future sale can be low. In addition, where you are borrowing to buy such an apartment, some lenders may have restrictions around lending for property which is under a certain size, and you should check with your lender before moving too far ahead with such a purchase.

Student accommodation

With the rise in student numbers in developed countries worldwide, and many of those students coming from countries with substandard education, there has become a need to house this growing population. Throughout the world there are many iterations of student accommodation, and in some countries individual investors can buy them for the purposes of generating an income.

Depending upon the country in which you are investing, student accommodation can take a few forms, including:

- purpose-built apartments that are decked out suitably for students, close to major universities – these are often very small and may contain a kitchenette and small ensuite as well as a study nook

- houses where there are up to eight bedrooms, each with a bathroom, plus a common room and kitchen

- regular houses that someone has previously rented out (or will rent out in the future) as single rooms to individual students.

Some 'experts' are today teaching the concept of buying standard housing near universities to lease to individual students. While this may work to create a good income stream, thought must be given to the considerable additional hassles when you have so many students in the one property. It may not be possible to get a property manager who would be happy to take on this more complex arrangement and you may well find yourself saddled with the task of self-management. With so many students in the one house there are bound to be a lot of extra problems and you may cease to enjoy a quiet existence if you own such a property!

In the main, I don't recommend embracing the student market as a good strategy for creating positive cash flow property, unless you have the time needed to oversee your property closely.

WHAT ARE THE ISSUES?

All niche-market property is at risk of failing to deliver a suitable return when used for its original purpose. Hotels may suffer high vacancy, poor management or an oversupply. Over-55s communities may be built in the wrong place, and struggle to find tenants. Student accommodation lends itself to an oversupply, with many new complexes around universities coming onto the market. The added problems that come with renting property to young people may make you sorry you ever proceeded. In a nutshell, you could end up with a far worse income stream than you had hoped, and far more issues than you had anticipated.

Does this mean that you should steer clear of niche-market property? Not necessarily, but it does mean that extra care must be taken. The credentials of any on-site manager must be thoroughly examined. The need for student accommodation should be confirmed by university enrolment numbers. The popularity of an area with seniors must be clarified by your demographic research.

Most importantly, you must ensure that there is a second end use for that niche-market property, so that you incorporate a safety net. If you buy an apartment in a hotel, be sure it is a suite with a bedroom, bathroom and kitchen and not just a hotel room. That way, you can always lease it to a longer-term tenant as a one-bedroom apartment. Make sure that the student accommodation and seniors' apartment or villa can be turned into ordinary apartments with little cost, so that you can easily make the change if required. Check with local government that there are no restrictions on using the property in a way that is different to its original purpose, as there may be a covenant that prevents you from making the change.

Lastly, of course, be sure that it is priced at market value. Don't pay more for it than you would otherwise pay for a standard residential property, just because the potential income looks so good. If, at some time in the future, you do need to convert the property to standard housing, you will definitely be getting a smaller return. You don't want to find yourself holding a property with a highly negative cash flow.

SUMMARY

Niche-market properties carry a significant risk, much higher than standard residential. If you are buying such a property your research needs to be even more accurate and your timing must be good. If you do feel that a niche-market property is a suitable asset for you, and you believe you have found a likely property in an area that has a great prognosis for growth, ensure that you have the capacity to lose money if the asset does not perform as hoped.

QUESTION TWELVE

Does this property match your personal risk profile?

If you decided that you wanted to invest in shares or managed funds, it's unlikely that you would just go online and choose a suitable investment all on your own. Few people have the skills to sort through the many options, and many people don't have the financial literacy to even understand how it all works.

Thus, you would probably seek out the advice of a qualified financial adviser. Financial advisers have a series of legal obligation to ensure that the recommendations they make for you are appropriate. Unlike property spruikers, they can't just recommend an investment to you because it gives them a good rate of commission.

At the first consultation, the adviser would start by asking you to complete a personal risk profile. The purpose of this profile is to determine your capacity to manage risk, and to guide the financial adviser towards recommending suitable products for you. If, for example, your risk profile showed that you might be risk-averse, the adviser would most probably recommend that your money be placed in assets that carry little risk, such as government bonds and fixed-interest securities. A person showing a profile that embraced risk, by contrast, might be ready to invest in a shares-based portfolio, and perhaps even in futures and other commodities.

What you must understand about buying property is that this assessment of risk is equally important. As you have seen from the information that I have provided to you so far, not all property is equal and nor are all areas. The problem with buying property from someone who claims to be a 'property expert' is that they will probably not ask you a single question about your attitude to risk! The property they recommend to you will come from a list of properties to which they have access, rather than from a list that they have put together as a result of asking you a series of questions about risk.

One of the biggest problems with the lack of regulation in the property investment industry is that there are far too many unqualified people providing advice to investors, making property recommendations without ever pausing to consider the risk profile of the buyer. As a result, every day people are buying property that is not right for them and then spending the following years worrying because it is either not performing or is at high risk of something going wrong. They may emerge unhappy with the outcome and wishing they had never taken the plunge in the first place.

At this point in the 20 Must Ask Questions®, it's time to assess your personal risk profile. Then, measure the risk rating of the types of property you have chosen, and ensure that you are looking at property that fits best with your profile. Once you have done this, you will realise that any property outside of the risk rating you have given to yourself is one that you should not consider, no matter how good it might look on paper!

YOUR PROPERTY RISK PROFILE

The financial advice industry has a fairly standard risk profile upon which most individual advisers base their own risk analysis. Usually, this risk profile questionnaire seeks to identify the investment areas that most suit your capacity to withstand risk. It will ask you a range of questions that are designed to place you somewhere along the risk continuum, and then list the assets that offer a degree of risk that matches your tolerance.

Assets are measured for risk in terms of their ability to return your capital, their ability to grow your capital and their ability to generate income for you. Assets that grow the least and return the smallest amount in income, yet are most likely to preserve capital, will be recommended to risk-averse people. Assets that have the capacity to grow incredibly and return high levels of income, yet carry a high risk of loss of capital, will be recommended to investors with the highest risk profiles. All other assets will rate somewhere in between these two extremes.

A property risk profile is a little different from this. It is not designed to assess *if* property is the right asset class for you. It assumes that this has already been determined, or that you have made the independent choice to invest in property because you feel it is right for you. A property risk profile does not suggest that property is better or worse than other options (and nor do I). It is simply designed to show you that some types of property carry more or less risk than others and that, as a prudent investor, you should only ever choose types that suit your identified risk profile.

A good example of how the varying characteristics of different kinds of property affect how risky they are is commercial property. It seems to be a fairly attractive option, because it can have higher returns than residential property. In most cases, the tenant pays the outgoings – such as property taxes, rates, and repairs and maintenance – and tenants often have significantly longer leases than in residential. So, it would seem that buying a commercial property would be a far smarter idea than buying a residential house.

What needs to be known, though, is that commercial property has higher returns because it has higher risk. Those risks include a higher vacancy rate, and for longer periods. It has many more risks too, and I'll outline those in this chapter. An investor should only buy it if it suits their risk profile – otherwise they will be uncomfortable with the choice and potentially severely financially distressed if one of the risks materialises.

I have personally witnessed just how devastating it can be to buy a property which is not suitable for your risk profile. The building where my office is situated was 65 per cent vacant for three years after completion, with the only occupants being owner-occupiers such as ourselves. The remaining vacant offices were owned by investors, two of them being retirees needing to see income from their investment. I felt incredibly sorry for these people, many of whom were forced to sell. If only they had completed a risk profile before deciding to buy!

Since no-one has ever developed a property risk profile in Australia (to my knowledge), I decided to produce one of my own. Again, let me stress that this risk profile doesn't determine whether property is the right asset for you – to determine that, you may like to complete a standard investment risk profile. This questionnaire assumes you know that property of some kind is right for your personal needs, and you want to further narrow down which property *type* is suitable for you.

You can find a copy of it at the end of this book. Complete the profile, and you will know a little more about your attitude to risk when it comes to exposure, income and growth, and the property types that then suit this attitude. Then read on for a summary of the features of each type of property, and how I rate the risk of each. You will then know which property types are most suited to you.

STANDARD RESIDENTIAL PROPERTY

A standard residential property is a property which exists in a city, suburb or town and is let out for someone to live permanently within. This includes houses, apartments, villas and duplexes which offer longer-term leases.

Positive features

- If you follow the 20 Questions closely when buying, you have a high chance of seeing consistent returns, because these 20 Questions eliminate some of the risk by checking on demand and supply factors.

- This kind of property will always retain some value, usually at least what you have paid for it. It is unlikely to be worth less than you paid, unless you bought in an overheated market or at auction or you ignored the 20 Questions and made no effort to establish whether there was demand for the property or not. If you bought in an overheated market or paid too much, then time should smooth this out.

- It is accepted as security for borrowing to a maximum of 95 per cent (although more commonly only up to 90 per cent). Note that this fact changes from time to time and from country to country, with some countries having a maximum amount that you can borrow if you are borrowing for investment purposes.

- It generally rises in value over time, creating the ability to leverage. The time it takes to increase in value will depend on a whole host of factors, as covered in this book.

- You can quite easily insure against some contingent losses (e.g. rent, house and contents, building) using landlord's insurance and building insurance.

Negative features

- In the event that you face an emergency requiring access to funds, it cannot be quickly turned into cash, although it is possible to put in place a loan against equity if you qualify. Even then, though, unless you have built in a margin when you borrowed to buy the property, increasing a loan to access cash can take weeks, and even months, to be put in place.

- Vacancy can put a strain on your cash flow (although positive cash flow will help you manage this risk). If you experience more vacancy than you had estimated when you calculated your cash flows, you could be put into a position where you are forced to sell; or worse, where you have not been keeping up your loan repayments, you may face a mortgagee sale.

- Tenants can cause damage or even flee without paying the rent. However, landlord's insurance can ensure that your losses from an event like this are minimal. Even then, many landlord's insurance policies have a cap on claims and on the length of time rent will be paid if a property is unable to be tenanted due to damage, and you may end up footing the bill for the ongoing expenses on a property, without any corresponding rent to help you manage them.

- You may buy in an area that either loses value or does not gain value as quickly as other areas. This can happen even when you ask the 20 Questions, which may uncover growth drivers but which cannot determine the time frame within which that growth may happen.

Risk rating

The risk of residential property compared to other classes of investment is low to medium: closer to the low side if you find positive or neutral cash flow. Compared with other property types it is low in risk.

COMMERCIAL PROPERTY

A commercial property is any property that has been zoned by the local government as commercial, industrial or retail, and is leased for the purposes of running a business of some type. This can include shops, offices, warehouse, storage facilities and factories.

Positive features

- You may achieve a higher rate of return for the money you spend, as returns can be around 10 per cent of the purchase price.

- Since the values and rents are intrinsically linked, the value of the property usually increases when the rent increases.

- A good commercial property with a long-term tenant can be easier to sell than a residential property.

- Tenants are required to 'make good' on the property at the end of the lease, meaning they are required to return it to a condition or state outlined in the contract.

Negative features

- Your commercial property is likely to attract small business owners, as larger businesses very often own their own property. The failure rate for small business is high, with some estimates claiming that it may be as high as 80 per cent. Statistically speaking, this means that you have a high chance of getting tenants who will not see out their lease!

- Often, the landlord must offer incentives in order to attract a tenant, such as free fit-out or rent-free periods. This adds to the expense bottom line and reduces the value of the relative rent.

- Commercial property has a markedly higher rate of vacancy than residential property and can be vacant for much longer periods.

- Commercial property is affected by both the tenancy market and the general state of the economy, as the tenant's business will suffer when the economy is performing poorly. Where it is situated in an area where the population is diminishing, there is an increased risk of vacancy.

Risk rating

The risk of investing in commercial property is considered to be medium when compared to other investment vehicles, and medium to high when compared with other property types.

HOLIDAY (VACATION) HOUSES AND APARTMENTS MANAGED BY A PROPERTY MANAGER

This is a category which is well represented all over the world. It can be represented by any houses or apartments you decide to lease on a short-term basis through a local holiday (vacation) property manager, an on-site caretaker or Airbnb. Such properties may or may not already be leased in this fashion when you buy them.

Positive features

- Well-chosen property, suitable for short-term tenants and situated in a popular area, will let frequently and can provide a very large positive cash flow, particularly when new, as they often have an abundance of on-paper deductions (in countries where these are allowed). New apartments can benefit from even more on-paper deductions, because where a deduction for loss of value applies, it is given to you on your share of any common areas as well as on the property you own.

- A holiday property showing a strong history of good returns will be relatively liquid, as the demand for such property may be high.

- If the area remains popular, the increasing rental returns will impact positively on capital growth. Some destinations remain popular for many years, and if you have purchased your property early enough (before the prices became too high), you will enjoy many years of positive cash flow and a strong growth in value.

- Some investors see as a benefit the fact that you can use the property yourself for your own vacation or at weekends, when it doesn't have a booking. Be careful with this though – if you are using your property at times when it could be reasonably expected that a booking could be received, you may be required to make an adjustment on your tax return for personal use, meaning that you will have a reduced capacity to claim the expenses incurred when earning an income. This can usually be managed by ensuring that the property remains 'available' for rent at all times, and it is only used by the owner at the last minute when a booking is no longer feasible.

Negative features

- If you have a property with an on-site manager who is responsible for leasing out individual properties under their management, and where all properties in that particular complex are the same, you are relying on that manager to let out your property on a fair, rotational basis with other properties they manage. You cannot guarantee that this will occur.

- A holiday or vacaction home manager must be able to incur expenses on your behalf, as tenants turn around regularly (often weekly or even daily). These costs can be high and ultimately come out of your rental return, and they may not be managed as well as you would manage them yourself.

- Management costs can be higher for the vacation rental market than for residential property – up to 12–20 per cent.

- You cannot be watching the manager every minute of the day, so you actually have very little control over the arrangement.

- If the holiday arrangement is not delivering results and you need to change the property to become a standard residential one, this may be difficult where the property itself is not suitable for long-term renting – for example, if there is not a proper kitchen or if it is too small.

Risk rating

The risk of investing in a holiday (vacation) house is medium when compared to other investment vehicles, and medium when compared with other property types.

HOTELS, RESORTS AND SERVICED AND MANAGED APARTMENTS

These types of properties are usually strata, corporate, condominium or community titled, and the apartment owners hand over control to another entity that runs a business in their collective property. They became popular in the 1990s and early 2000s as large hotel chains tried to profit from selling off their main assets (their buildings) by individually titling the rooms and apartments and selling them to everyday investors.

Positive features

- Often there is a bar, a conference room and so on, in the complex. These make up part of the common property, of which you own a piece, and in countries which allow deductions for on-paper depreciation, you will obtain all the relevant deductions (pro rata for your proportion).

- Managers are sometimes paid a percentage of the profits as an income, rather than a set fee, as an incentive to operate as profitably as possible.

- In countries where there is a higher degree of depreciation available on tourism property, the amount of positive cash flow can be very high and will often provide a hedge against vacancy or lower than expected returns.

Negative features

- A poorly performing manager means less income for you.

- The costs of running an entire hotel-style operation, as opposed to simply letting out apartments, may blow the budget, although this can be grounds for dismissal of the manager by the responsible entity.

- If the hotel is seasonal you may have downtime when there is little income. (This applies to any tourism investment.)

- Forecast net returns have been found in the past to be unachievable on some properties.

- Oversupply of similar property in the area can have a devastating impact on your return.

- It can be difficult to find a lender who will provide funds to buy these types of properties, due to their size, the nature of the tenancy and the low-demand resale.

Risk rating

The risk of investing in a managed apartment is medium to high when compared to other investment vehicles, and high when compared with other property types. The reason for the high rating is that if you choose an area that subsequently does not enjoy success as a tourist destination, you will have low occupancy without a corresponding lowering of costs (as hotels and resorts have a lot of fixed costs). You also face the added risks of, firstly, poor management and, secondly, the economy in general impacting negatively on tourism. Finally, when it comes time to sell, this type of property can be harder to sell, especially if the performance has been poor or mediocre.

WHAT IS BEST FOR YOU IN THE AREA YOU HAVE FOUND?

Go back to your list of the areas and property types you have examined so far. In the areas you have been looking, is the type of property for which there is the most demand also in a category that matches your risk profile? If so, proceed further. If not, take the area off your list and do more research on some of your other choices.

You might now like to sort the areas and property types you have chosen into a priority list, with the areas containing property most unlike your personal risk profile at the bottom of the list.

It's likely that most people will make the independent choice that a normal residential property in an area which satisfies the 20 Questions is what they want to buy, at least first up. However, at some point in your investing life the opportunity for a different kind of property will more than likely present itself to you. Keep in mind your risk profile and be sure you stay true to it before plunging ahead with a property that may not suit you.

RISK WHEN INVESTING WITH OTHERS

You may be in a situation where you decide that you will invest with someone else. This could be your life partner, or it may be a sibling, friend or a group of other people who are pooling their funds to be able to amplify their investing opportunity.

Where you are investing with a life partner, the most important thing to be aware of is that you may both have a different attitude to risk. One of you may be risk-averse while the other is comfortable with it. As you can guess, this leads to one of two things happening: either you will continue to disagree with each other, and perhaps never get around to actually buying a property, or one of you will win and the other will spend the entire period of investment unhappy, or stressed, about that purchase.

It is critical that, before you even begin the search for an investment property, you sit down with each other and discuss your attitudes to risk. Complete the risk profile separately, and then establish whether you feel the same about risk, or whether there is a significant gap in your expectations. This situation may require some compromise on both sides in order for you to be able to begin investing. Where one party is severely risk-averse, it could be that property investing is not a suitable vehicle for your financial plans.

While a similar situation can occur where you are investing with siblings or other people, and it also needs to be managed in the same way, a further risk exists in that case.

You see, regardless of how fabulous your relationship is with your siblings and friends, you are individuals with often vastly different financial situations. Some of the ways that you may differ include:

- different time horizons, leading to a disagreement about when to disinvest

- different capacity to borrow, meaning obtaining a loan could be difficult if one party cannot demonstrate capacity to repay their share

- alternative ideas about what to buy, who to rent it to and whether to renovate or not

- vastly different personal financial circumstances – and this could lead to one party suffering financial distress, rendering them unable to support their part of the equation, leaving the remaining people with the ongoing financial obligation of the property.

The other issue which arises when you borrow money to buy an investment with other people is that you are all jointly and severally responsible for that debt. If someone suddenly decided to no longer be a part of the investment, and stopped supporting their portion of the commitment, the lender would pursue the remaining parties. This is an outcome which may eventuate where that person had other obligations which they failed to meet (say, other loans not associated with the property they share with you) and other lenders subsequently pursue them for payment. In that situation, you may be forced to sell the property to satisfy that person's other debts, and this could be long before the property has had a chance to deliver any kind of positive performance.

There is one more risk that you may encounter when you decide to invest with people who are not your life partner – and that is one of future capacity to buy property without them. The property you buy jointly may grow exceptionally well, and you may wish to leverage against that growth to invest further. Unless that other party also agrees, you may be prevented from doing so. You also cannot use equity owned with someone else to invest on your own unless they are willing, and have the capacity, to become a guarantor. Even if you had a cash deposit of your own, or equity in another property, and wanted to buy additional properties without those other people, you may be limited in doing so, because the commitment to the entire loan you have with those other people is considered by the bank to be solely yours when it comes to assessing your capacity to service a further debt. In short, you may be able to afford to borrow more, but your commitment with those other people may get in the way.

Investing with others carries many risks over and above the inherent risks that property itself carries, and you should think carefully before agreeing to enter such an arrangement.

YOUR PROFILE MAY CHANGE!

As you add property to your portfolio and become more confident in what you are doing, it is highly likely that your risk profile may change. You may start out being risk-averse, but as you begin to see that the experience of buying property doesn't carry all of the drawbacks you had imagined, you begin to embrace risk a little more fervently.

You should revisit your risk profile at least every 12 months, or every time you add a property to your portfolio. Doing so will ensure that you are always obtaining properties which match your risk profile and not missing out on any opportunities which may arise.

SUMMARY

Your risk profile is an extremely important part of choosing where and what to buy. In doing your research you may come across an area or property type that seems to have exceptional returns. However, unless your personal profile supports your investment into this area or property, you should avoid the temptation, as this investment would likely cause stress to you.

You should now flick through to the end of this book and complete the risk profile questionnaire, if you haven't already, and then adjust your list as necessary before proceeding with the next question.

QUESTION THIRTEEN

What financing arrangements can you access for this property?

In *How to Achieve Property Success*, I have comprehensively explored financing options for property investors. By reading that book you will be not only equipped to effectively manage the entire process of investing, including everything you need to know before you begin and all of those post-purchase considerations, but you will better understand the options available to you when it comes time to get a loan. In addition to that, it covers the best types of loans to get for an investment property, how to use the loans to extract the greatest possible advantage and pay the minimum possible interest, and how to structure them so that you maximise every tax advantage available and pay off the debt quickly. The book also covers financing arrangements for different property types in detail. Please refer that book if you do not already have this type of information, as it is important.

This question isn't about how to borrow money and what type of loan you should get. It is more about preparing you to understand how the bank may view the different property types that you may choose, and whether you have any chance of even obtaining finance to buy the property which is likely to be in your sights at this stage of the process. It covers the *types* of security a bank is prepared to lend upon, and to what extent it may be prepared to lend. It would be a wasted exercise to go through the entire 20 Questions, find a property that you feel fits all the criteria, and then discover that there isn't a bank or financial institution that will lend money to you to buy it!

THE AREA OR TOWN

It's more than likely that the property you have chosen is a standard residential property. If that's the case, lending should be relatively straightforward, subject to a range of conditions. If you have decided that you are a higher-risk investor and, as such, have identified a niche-market property to buy, then things can be a little more complicated, as outlined below.

In *addition* to rules around the type of property for which a bank or lender will provide a loan, all lenders have specifications around how much they will lend, or whether they will lend at all, in certain areas.

For example, some of the major lenders have a minimum population requirement before they will lend for a purchase in an area. Where the area you are targeting is a suburb of a major city, this is usually not a concern, because it will be the population of the entire city that is considered. However, where it is a regional area or smaller town, there is likely to be minimum population criteria that some lenders will apply before they will agree to a loan. This minimum will vary from country to country and even from state to state and lender to lender. It could be that areas with a population under 7,000 are excluded by major lenders but included for smaller, regional lenders.

Other lenders may advance funds for purchases in towns and areas smaller than that, but only if a valuer can travel to the town to value the property. Be aware that under these circumstances, the cost to you to have the property valued will most probably be greater than the standard fee that most lenders will charge. You may well be paying for travel and accommodation for the valuer if the area is remote. I guess that means that buying in Betoota, Queensland (population -1, but there is a pub) or Oodnadatta, South Australia (population 230) is probably out of the question!

LOAN TO VALUATION RATIO (LVR)

The amount of the value of a property that you can obtain as a loan not only varies from property type to property type, it can also vary from area to area. In higher-risk areas, a lender may choose to continue lending, but at lower LVRs, requiring you as the borrower to take on more of the risk with a higher deposit (or more equity from other property). This is another factor that you must find out about before proceeding too far with the 20 Questions in any particular area.

THE LENDER'S EXPOSURE

In addition to population requirements, some lenders will have a maximum exposure that they are comfortable taking in an area even where the population is greater than the minimum criteria they may have applied. It is not unheard of for a lender to decide to provide no further lending once they already hold security over a certain number of properties in any one area. In addition, some lenders stop lending altogether in areas they deem high risk (such as a mining town), regardless of the population. They may or may not recommence lending at a time in the future when the risk is deemed to have passed.

This attitude to exposure can also apply to the lender's exposure to a particular development, such as a high-rise apartment block, apartments in a resort or a new land release. Many lenders do not like to take more than, say, a 15–20 per cent exposure to the one development, especially where that development is built in an area that may not yet have the runs on the board.

It can be a good idea to contact a broker before you do too much work on any property situated outside of major cities or towns. We have found that we have been able to save our clients a lot of time and hard work because we understand the level of exposure that all lenders will apply and can stop an investor going too far on a property that they have no chance of obtaining the loan to buy.

Let's now take a look at the property types you may be considering and explore the financing options for them.

STANDARD RESIDENTIAL HOUSES

Standard residential housing on freehold title in areas with a suitable population will normally qualify for the maximum available loan offered by most lending institutions, subject to you being able to satisfy borrowing criteria relating to your capacity to repay the debt. This 'serviceability' criteria changes all the time and so while you may have the go-ahead to buy a property from the bank, by the time you select one things may be different and you may no longer qualify.

In most countries you can borrow up to 80 per cent of the value of a property without paying lender's mortgage insurance. Lender's mortgage insurance, also known as private mortgage insurance, is an insurance policy to protect the lender in the event that you, the borrower, default and it cannot recover the full loan by selling the house. You pay the premium for the policy.

If you wish to borrow more than 80 per cent, you can usually do so, with approval. In many countries, you can borrow up to 90 per cent for an investment property and 95 per cent for an owner-occupied property.

The higher the LVR, the more expensive the loan costs, regardless of the underlying security, as mortgage insurance kicks in. In many countries, higher LVRs also carry much higher interest rates. In some countries the borrowing criteria becomes stricter as you borrow higher amounts, but in others the risk to the lender is simply reflected in a higher interest rate.

The premium for mortgage insurance is based on both the percentage you wish to borrow (LVR), and the size of the loan. So, a large loan will be more expensive than a small loan. A large loan with a high LVR will be more expensive than both a smaller loan and the same size loan with an LVR closer to 80 per cent.

APARTMENTS

In most cases, apartments intended for standard residential letting will fall under the same borrowing rules as standard houses. If, however, the total size of the apartment is small (for example, less than 50 square metres in Australia), the loan amount available will more likely be closer to 50 per cent of the total value or purchase price. Some lenders will not advance any funds for such purchases. This is because in the past, banks have found it very hard to re-sell property of such a small size, and so the risk to them is greater.

As outlined previously, apartments, especially those in high-rises, will often fall under the exposure rules of a lender, and each lender may only be willing to take an exposure to a percentage of the total security.

VACANT LAND

While it is unlikely that you will be considering vacant land, some investors are prepared to tread the somewhat treacherous route of land banking, or developing a property themselves. Having tried this – and bearing the scars to prove it – I recommend against it, especially if you are a busy person or if you are a relatively inexperienced investor. If you are set on pursuing this option, you will usually be able to borrow up to 95 per cent of the value of standard vacant land, under the same conditions as residential houses. Rural land has different borrowing rules in different countries – for example, in Australia, a maximum of 70 per cent can be borrowed, and no lender's mortgage insurance is allowed.

SERVICED APARTMENTS

Earlier in this book I discussed various kinds of niche-market properties (see Question Eleven). Serviced apartments are usually found in resorts or hotels, and have tenancy arrangements which are short-term, usually overnight or a minimum of two nights. Few lenders like serviced apartments, because their history is chequered – there has been a substantial number of failed ventures where owners have been left without a tenant (remember Chris, earlier?).

However, if the apartment can easily be used for standard residential accommodation (that is, if it is large enough to be turned into a long-term let apartment), and it is in an area where there is not an oversupply, some lenders may advance funds for a purchase of this nature. As this is usually considered an 'out of policy' lend, approvals are granted on a case-by-case basis.

RETIREMENT COMMUNITY PROPERTY

The world has an ageing population. With advances in medical science, people are staying alive longer. Many are retiring early. Due to this good health, combined with the desire of many older people to stay active and to be part of a community, we are seeing more and more retirement communities spring up all over the world, most often in warm climates.

The issue is that the very nature of a retirement-community apartment or villa is that it is small, often only around 35 square metres (more like a large hotel apartment). To combat the problems that buyers always have with borrowing to buy these apartments, some clever developers include two apartments for every one title, in a 'dual key' type arrangement. This means that the bank is getting in excess of the required 50 square metres as security, and the investor is getting two incomes. The developer, of course, gets the sale!

Regardless of this trick, many lenders do refuse to provide lending for the purchase of retirement-community properties. This is most likely because resale on these kinds of properties are still not as strong as for standard residential properties and they don't tend to grow as well. You should check with your lender or speak to your broker before considering such a property.

HOTEL ROOMS

While many countries have moved toward dividing up the titles of former hotels and selling the rooms off to investors (or building new hotels or holiday apartments for the purposes of selling to investors), lenders have been slow to embrace the concept. There are a few reasons for this. Firstly, they are small and do not satisfy the minimum size criteria. Secondly, they can be difficult to turn into standard apartments if the hotel fails. Thirdly, they have a history of having poor resale value, likely because the market for them is small.

As such, it can be hard to find a lender who will advance funds for this kind of purchase and investors then find themselves with no choice but to access equity they may have elsewhere, or use their own cash, if they wish to buy these. The issue then becomes that, even if the property *does* grow in value, the investor is not able to leverage against that growth to buy more property because the lender will continue to refuse to accept it as security for further borrowing.

STUDENT ACCOMMODATION

As outlined in Question Five, in some university towns developers complete projects that are purpose-built for students. The theory is that income on these is higher, since you can fit in more students, or the smaller apartments get a higher-rental return for their size than ordinary apartments can. In real life it rarely pans out this way, though: there are higher periods of vacancy, especially during school holidays or university breaks.

Most lenders will not accept purpose-built student accommodation as security. Some will accept accommodation where students are tenants, as long as it has other possible uses.

COMMERCIAL PROPERTY

Most of the questions contained in this book can apply equally well to the purchase of commercial property, as they relate to an area and the potential ability of that area to provide investing success to you. In most countries, the maximum loan available for a commercial property is usually 70 per cent of its value and this is a reflection of the higher-risk nature of commercial property of any type. The terms and conditions of a commercial loan are different, too, and usually the interest rate will be slightly higher, again because the bank recognises that there is a slightly higher risk to these types of properties.

THINGS CAN CHANGE

The lending criteria of every lender, in every country, are fluid and change often without notice. Equally, your own capacity to borrow changes as you add more properties (and therefore more risk) to your own situation. You may have been led to believe that you can borrow 'x' amount of money but, by the time you submit a loan application, this may have changed vastly.

It's important to build a strong relationship with a bank or broker, making sure that the person you are dealing with is educated about property investing. Then, keep abreast of the changes to lending criteria, interest rates, loan types and maximum LVRs so that you don't waste time finding a property to buy, only to find that you cannot find a lender to finance it.

RENT

When you borrow from a bank to buy a property, you want the bank to recognise the security and provide the maximum loan possible. You also want it to recognise the rent the property will provide as part of your assessable income, so that your capacity to borrow is increased. After all, when you are applying to borrow money, not only does the lender consider whether the security provided is solid, it considers whether your total income is sufficient to cover your ongoing loan commitment. When you buy an investment property, your expenses will increase, but so will your income.

Depending upon the country in which you are borrowing, a commonly accepted practice is for the lender to recognise 80 per cent of the rental income from standard residential property. Different kinds of property will have the rent or income accepted at different levels, depending upon the level of risk involved in that property type and where it is. The reason that a lender will most likely never accept 100 per cent of rental income is because they are taking into account the fact that that there may be periods of vacancy. In some countries, lenders will also recognise some of the tax deductions you will receive, such as that for loan interest. In other words, although you have a commitment to the interest accruing on the new investment debt, the lender's calculations may consider the fact that the loan repayment may be greater than the income (creating a claimable loss) and you will get back some of your tax. Therefore, the income the lender assesses as being received will be boosted by this tax break and added to your assessable income. In some way, this makes up for the fact that the bank may only accept 80 per cent of the rental income.

Example

Here is an example to explain how this works. Note that the tax amounts are not accurate – the example is for illustration purposes only.

Graeme earns $50,000 per annum and pays $10,000 in tax: a net income of $40,000. The property he wants to buy provides $10,000 in rent each year.

The bank adds $8,000 to his assessable income (80 per cent of the rent). His assessable income for borrowing purposes is therefore $58,000 gross.

However, as Graeme has substantial claims to make for both his actual property loss (as his expenses will exceed the rental income) and for his on-paper loss from depreciation, the bank makes consideration for the $14,000 in interest that Graeme will pay on the new investment debt, once approved. It knows that the tax office will only charge Graeme tax on his net income after his losses.

Although the lender will not make allowances for any tax claims other than those for loan interest, in Graeme's case it will allow a deduction of $14,000 (the loan interest) when calculating his net available income. Since it has assessed his gross income as $58,000, it subtracts the interest of $14,000 to arrive at an assessable income for tax purposes of $44,000.

The tax on $44,000 (in this example) is only $8,000. The bank then calculates as follows:

$58,000 (allowable income for assessment)

Less $8,000 (tax payable on reduced income)

Equals $50,000 assessable income for borrowing purposes.

In reality, Graeme earns $50,000, pays tax of $10,000 and gets rent of $10,000, making a net $50,000. So, even though the bank did its calculations based on 80 per cent of his rental income, its consideration of his reduced tax bill evens this out and makes his assessable income the same as his actual income!

Despite this calculation above, bear in mind that many lenders will only take at face value the rent less 20 per cent, and the tax breaks are not a consideration. Some banks will recognise less than 80 per cent of rental income. Where the rental income is from a hotel venture, possibly only 50 per cent will be allowed. The same applies for retirement-community property, if the bank agrees to accept that income at all.

WHEN THE BANK WON'T LEND ENOUGH

In rare circumstances, you may uncover a property that stacks up incredibly well against the entire 20 Questions but is considered to be outside of lending policy guidelines. For example, you may have found a serviced apartment that you believe has excellent prospects as holiday accommodation, and ample opportunity to attract long-term tenants if the hotel venture fails for some reason.

In the event that none of your preferred lenders will provide funding for a property that you have decided can work out well for you, and you are reluctant to explore alternative sources of funding, you may have enough equity in property elsewhere to fund the purchase.

As already mentioned, in most cases the bank will provide loans of up to 80 per cent without requiring lender's mortgage insurance. I also recommend you keep all of your borrowing below this 80 per cent level, as this will allow you to maintain

20 per cent ownership across your portfolio. This provides a buffer should you experience a property value plateau.

Since few people have enough cash savings to meet a 20 per cent shortfall plus the associated buying costs (approximately 5 per cent of the purchase price), many use equity that they own in property elsewhere as a deposit. For example, if your family home was valued at $200,000, the bank would allow a loan of $160,000. Thus, if the current debt on your home was, say, $90,000, you essentially would have $70,000 of available funds to put towards another property. If you found property to the value of, say, $300,000, the bank would advance $240,000 against the new property (80 per cent) and lend you $70,000 against your existing property. The $10,000 left over would pay your costs.

Some people have experienced exceptional growth on their family homes or have a considerable amount of investment property that has enjoyed good levels of growth. This means they have much more equity in property than the average person. From an equity point of view, the bank will usually provide $5 of loan funds for every $1 of equity you have, subject to you satisfying other lending criteria, including having sufficient income and rents to repay the debt. This means that if an investor had $1.5 million in equity, technically they could borrow five times that amount – $7.5 million! (Of course, it is most unlikely that this investor would qualify under the serviceability criteria for such a loan.)

So, people with this high level of equity may wish to consider using this to buy property that the bank will not accept as security. Since they have so much equity available in existing property, there may not be a need for the bank to take security over additional property. In other words, the investor can borrow the funds against already owned property and use that to buy the new, 'unacceptable' property. The investor, of course, then gets to hold the title to this new property, as it is not mortgaged. The interest on the loan acquired to buy this new property can still be claimed as a tax deduction, too, as it is the purpose for the loan that determines tax-deductibility, not what secures the debt.

Bear in mind that, if the bank will not accept a property as security, it is also unlikely to accept the income derived from this new property, at least at first. Sometimes in later years, when evidence of steady income can be produced by the owner, it becomes acceptable.

The main drawback to using equity to buy 'unacceptable' property is one of limiting leverage. If you use up your equity to borrow for a property that you cannot use as security, any increase in the value of that new property cannot be used to leverage into other purchases. You would have to wait until the property you own that *is* acceptable to the bank increases in value again to obtain more leveraging ability. Using a strategy such as this therefore requires careful consideration and an assessment of its true impact in future years. Remember, if the bank will not accept the property or its income, it may be for a good reason that you should perhaps heed.

SUMMARY

Not all banks will provide a loan for all properties in all areas, and not all loans are suitable for investing in property. If you haven't already looked into lending, and you would like to know more, read my book *How to Achieve Property Success* where an entire chapter is devoted to loan types, how to qualify and how to get the best available loan.

Now that you have an idea of what financing arrangements may be available on the types of property you are most likely to buy, let's move on to Question Fourteen.

QUESTION FOURTEEN

What is the market value?

Very few people understand the true meaning of 'market value'. When you see that your neighbour's house is for sale, how do you react? I bet, in most cases, you think to yourself, 'Well, if their property is worth that much, ours must be worth at least $20,000 more!' There seems to be a general perception that the value of a property is more tied up with its presentation and decor than its size and location.

In addition to the fact that decor and presentation do not have a huge impact on true market value, the value of a property is also not determined by the listed price of the properties around it, and 'market value' is not the listed price of houses similar to yours. Real estate agents are notorious for overstating prices to obtain listings, and subsequently talking the owners' expectations down as they become more desperate to sell.

I receive an abundance of email from people who tell me that every property they do calculations for has extremely negative cash flow. When I enquire further, I usually discover that the authors of these emails have been using the *listed* price to do their calculations! Whether you need to pay the price advertised or not depends very much on whether you are purchasing in a cold, warm or hot market.

MARKET TEMPERATURE

It is important that you understand the temperature of the market, as this will give you an idea of how well you will be able to negotiate.

Last year a client of mine had decided that there was a suburb in Melbourne where he really wanted to buy. He was a skilled negotiator and had purchased several properties well below their advertised price in other markets. He was tough as nails and refused to budge far from his opening bid.

He had asked the 20 Questions of this market and decided that it represented a great opportunity for him. So he found a few properties and began to negotiate. He had a particular formula that he had worked out that seemed to have good results – he would always start bidding 12 per cent under listed price and never get closer to listed price than 5 per cent below, walking away and onto the next property. In the past this had always resulted in him securing some great bargains.

This time though, he found himself walking away from property after property. After a few months he had become really annoyed, determined to get a bargain and becoming more fixed in his insistence to not be the one who folded and paid any more than his formula dictated.

The issue here was that, in his bid to stick to his negotiating formula, he had failed to consider the temperature of the market. In this case it was a very warm market indeed – and the fact that the 20 Questions stacked up so well should have told him that. Had he considered the supply/demand metrics more carefully, he would have noticed that there were considerably more people looking at this market than the average, and this alone spoke of a very warm market.

After I had spoken to him and explained that while he was refusing to budge off his own fixed formula the prices were actually going up, he quickly changed tack. Five months after he began searching, he secured a property at the price it was listed for. In the following months he enjoyed further capital growth on that property, and the rents also increased. It was a good buy.

It would have been a *better* buy if, instead of being stubborn about his approach to *how* he was going to buy, he had read the market more accurately and realised that it was a market which required an offer closer to listed price. It is highly likely that he would have secured a similar property to the one he eventually bought, but up to $30,000 cheaper, had he read this market correctly and bought before the prices began to increase in earnest.

I believe that the ability to negotiate is a critical skill that you must acquire as a property investor. Failure to negotiate well is the reason that a significant proportion of the property investing public pay more for a property than they need to. However, in addition to being able to negotiate well, you have to know what the market is doing so you know when to hold and when to fold. The supply/demand metrics that you uncovered in Question Five will give you an idea if you're moving in a cold market (i.e. there are lower than average numbers of people looking), a warm market (there is an average number of buyers looking) or a hot market (there are more buyers than the average).

Extremely cold markets should be considered speculative, and you should not buy in them unless you are happy to wait for growth (and realise that it may not come). If the market is that cold, however, very few of the criteria these questions spotlight are likely to be evident.

Extremely hot markets should be avoided, because it is likely you are too late. Where properties are being snapped up the moment they hit the market (or before, in off-market sales) then prices are likely to have already risen considerably.

Warm to very warm markets are the best to buy in, and how close to market value you need to make your offer will depend upon just how warm that market has become.

MARKET VALUE

When valuers are asked to perform a valuation on a property, they will spend a reasonable amount of time doing so. They will measure each room, take notes about the standard of inclusions and the condition of the property, and even consider the landscaping and alterations. Then, back in their office, they will search records to establish the prices paid in recent sales in the area.

I get a laugh every time I see the latest spruiker on TV or at a property expo claiming that their scheme of buying properties, spending minimal dollars on an aesthetic makeover and then selling them nets them profits in the tens of thousands, or even a hundred thousand, dollars. In many of the cases where a good increase in value was obtained, the increase was due in part to the makeover (with the amount of increase usually exactly matching what was spent on the upgrade) and in part to the fact that the property was bought just before a small boom took place! Without the boom, which would have affected all properties in that area, the increase in value would probably have been commensurate only with the spend on the upgrade.

True market value is the price that a property can fetch. When a property is sold, the price obtained becomes the benchmark market value for all properties of a similar size and quality in that area. Presentation and decoration only adds, or takes away, very small amounts, since aesthetic items such as impressive decor usually only add to saleability, not price. Let's say you owned an apartment in a block where all apartments were the same, and you had paid $380,000. If your neighbours subsequently sold their identical apartment for $350,000, the value of your apartment would become $350,000.

If you are seeking standard residential property in the areas you have researched thus far, ensure that you are familiar with market value. The listed prices will be above market value (in the hope that you will pay more), so you must discover for what price other similar properties in the area have recently sold. Go online, check auction results and if you need to, ask the agent to get you a list of the recent sales in the area. All agents have access to a database of sale prices in their region, and an enthusiastic sales agent should be willing to share this with you if you are a serious buyer.

MARKET VALUE FOR NICHE-MARKET PROPERTY

Checking that a property is at market value is especially crucial if you are buying a non-standard property like a serviced apartment, hotel apartment, retirement property or student accommodation. The history of how niche-market property in Australia has been valued will explain why.

In about 1996, when these types of properties were first released to the Australian market, developers decided to price them as one would price a commercial property. Commercial property is generally valued according to the yield it can achieve. For example, a shop in an area where yields are 10 per cent, which achieves a rent of $5,000 a month ($60,000 a year), would be valued at $600,000. If the rent were to increase to $5,500 a month ($66,000 a year) the value of the property would increase to $660,000.

Residential property is not valued in this way. If it were, and accepted residential rental yields were, say, 5 per cent, then all property with a rental return of $200 a week ($10,400 a year) would sell for $208,000.

Developers decided that many of these niche-market properties would need to achieve at least a 7.5 per cent yield to make them attractive, so they worked out prices that would deliver this yield. If, for example, a two-bedroom serviced apartment could fetch $200 a night for at least three nights a week ($600 a week or $31,200 per year), then at 7.5 per cent yield these properties would be valued and sold for $416,000. The problem was that, typically, a serviced apartment priced at

$416,000 would be situated in an area where properties of a comparable size available to long-term tenants were selling for only $250,000. The justification for the price was the higher return, but in the event that the hotel venture failed and these properties were converted to standard residential properties, a lot of money would instantly be lost – and too often was.

THOSE INVESTMENT CLUBS

As mentioned earlier in this book, property clubs have sprung up in Australia, under the guise of providing support and assistance to property investors in their endeavour to become financially secure. Other countries have similar associations or investor groups, all of which may operate differently from each other, yet which claim to have similar aims.

Where that club or group is a genuine gathering of interested investors who simply help each other to buy property, sharing research and information, they may be okay to be a part of, although without expert guidance sometimes the choices made by these groups can still be below par.

The clubs that I have an issue with, though, are those which are more organised, usually existing under registered company structures, and which are really just a front for a company which sells property that is *not* at market value to the members, who all think that they are part of a bona fide club of willing peers.

These 'clubs' purport to provide guidance and support from other investors who share with you an interest in property investing. This is believable, as the people who are retained to do these jobs are just as naive as the people they try to help. To give them credit, they really do believe they are providing assistance. From there, however, it becomes like every network marketing company, or 'relationship' marketing company as this system is now known, that has ever been in existence.

Property is sold to the members of the club, and the people at the top level make the profits. In the case of a few of these club arrangements in Australia, a 'loading' on the purchase price for marketing and support is declared, but this amount is well above standard real estate commissions. What they do not disclose is that, often, the properties are already inflated by up to 20 per cent before the loading is added! This 20 per cent is then carefully siphoned to the founders of the company. I personally know of at least four cases where properties offered to investors belonging to such a club were considerably more expensive than equivalent properties in the next street.

It is incredibly easy to avoid being in this situation. Find out what has recently sold in the area, and if necessary, pay for an independent valuation to be done on the property you are offered. That may cost you a few hundred dollars, but it may well save you 500 times that amount. If the property remains viable after you have answered this question and the other 19 questions, then it may be suitable to buy.

As a potential investor in any area and in any type of property, you will want to be very clear about the market value of similar property. Where the property is niche market, compare it to standard residential, as there is a good chance that this is what it will have to become in the future. Knowing what the real values are in an area will give you a good benchmark on which to base your negotiations, and will help you to know when to stop negotiating because the price has exceeded what the property is worth.

SUMMARY

Knowing the market value of a property and the market temperature of an area is a critical part of this process. You can make money right from the outset when buying a property, but only if you can secure a property at or, better still, below market value. Paying over market value will set you back and you will use those first months and years of growth simply getting back to square one. Once you know the market value, you're ready to move onto the next question.

QUESTION FIFTEEN

What are the specifics of the property itself?

As you get closer to the final questions in this process, you should now have a reasonable idea of the type of property you are most likely to buy, and the area in which you would like to buy it. You should know whether a lender will finance it and the target market in terms of tenants, and you will have a fair idea of what is presently on the market.

It is at this point that you are likely to begin narrowing down the actual properties that you wish to buy. You will make a shortlist and begin to consider the offers that you will make on those properties.

In the prior question we looked at market value and market temperature. You must know the market value in the area so that you get an idea of the price you are aiming for, and market temperature so that you know how much lower than the market value you can begin to negotiate. In addition to this, the price you are prepared to pay and how far under market value that price is will be linked to features of the property itself – and its structural condition.

Even if the property you are about to buy is relatively young, and potentially under a builder's warranty, you still need to know more detail about its structural condition. The more detail you can get, the stronger you become in the negotiation phase.

RESIDENTIAL HOUSES OR APARTMENTS

If you build a house yourself there will be a warranty which is provided by the builder to cover you for structural issues. If the property you are researching is already built but is still almost new, it will still have some form of builder's warranty attached to it and it will still be in force even if that house changes hands. In Australia the term of that warranty is six years. In the US the term is up to 20 years on the structure. Canada offers various terms with up to 10 years for structural defects.

While each country, and sometimes state within each country, has a different rule, generally there is a compulsory period of structural guarantee that all builders must provide to home-buyers – the builder is obliged by law to warrant their building materials and work. This warranty is transferable when the property changes hands, as it belongs to the building, not the owner.

In a nutshell, the warranty covers the soundness of the completed house or apartment. It requires that, during the warranty period, the builder must make good any defect whatsoever that is deemed to be a result of poor workmanship. All builders undertaking contracts of more than an amount set by the authorities ($5,000 in Australia) must also provide home warranty insurance before beginning work, to protect the owner in the event that they go broke or die while completing the project. This means that even smaller renovation projects are covered by home warranty insurance.

As a new owner of a property built within this warranty period, or one with renovations carried out within this period, you must know to whom you can refer any issues that you may have.

BUILDING A NEW HOME

If you have purchased a block of land, or have bought a house you intend to either demolish or rebuild, or to which you wish to add another dwelling, you will also, at some stage, be looking for a builder to complete the project for you. Selecting the right builder is about more than just going for the builder who can provide you with the cheapest quote – and so it is your responsibility to find out as much as you possibly can about the builder.

Firstly, you need to ask to be shown examples of work recently completed by that builder. Ask if you can speak to past clients to validate their satisfaction. This is the best way to establish that the product delivered to you will be of a standard and quality that will be immediately habitable, rather than in need of early repair and maintenance that could result in lost rent. It will also help you to find out whether the builder was easy to deal with and whether they delivered the completed build within the agreed price.

You also want to know if the company has a history of completing its projects in a timely fashion and ensure you have a fixed-time contract. When time frames blow out and you are left paying expenses – including possible loan interest – with no income from rent, the overall cost of the project increases, the cash flow decreases and the profit margins shrink. Timely building work is a critical factor when building a new home. Just be aware, though, that these contracts do specify numerous conditions under which the builder cannot be held responsible for a delay and someone else can be blamed for it – and in the building game, there is always someone else who can be blamed!

When we built a house behind another we had owned in Perth, I thought that, since we were employing a 'project home builder' and building almost exactly to the original plan, it would be a task that I could easily manage. We had a fixed term (26 weeks) and a fixed-price contract. I had established that we could support the interest on the progress payments we had to make for the six months it would take to build and that the final project cost, with that interest capitalised, would result in a profit to me.

Fourteen months passed, and I was still pushing the builder to complete. The fine print in the contract allowed him to blame all of the suppliers for the delay, and the additional $10,000 I paid on the 'fixed-price contract' was put down to extras that were not covered by the contract. The cost to us was not only the extra $10,000, but the additional interest on the almost fully drawn loan (the biggest progress payments are always the first few, meaning you're paying interest without income early on) during the additional eight months it took to build. The emotional stress was probably worth millions!

Read your contract thoroughly. Get someone with some legal knowledge to check it and explain it to you. I am of the opinion that there is really no such thing as a fixed-price/fixed-term contract, as the exclusions are simply too broad. Being prepared and building in a decent margin on all costs will ensure that you are not suddenly left with a project for which you paid too much, get too little rent and started behind on from day one.

BUYING OFF-THE-PLAN

When a developer undertakes a large project, they will attempt to get as many pre-sales as possible. Being able to secure promises to buy the finished stock, guaranteed with what is usually a significant deposit, often helps the developer to gain the construction finance they need to complete the project – with lenders happier to advance funds if they know that a substantial percentage of the finished stock is already under contract.

Thus, when you buy one of these off-the-plan (pre-construction) properties you will be asked to sign an unconditional contract and pay a deposit. The amount of this deposit can vary, but typically it is 10–20 per cent of the purchase price. Some investors use deposit bonds to pay this amount. A deposit bond or guarantee is offered in many countries and is a guarantee from an insurance company that, if the contract fails to finalise, it will meet the obligation to pay the 10 per cent that is forfeited to the developer or vendor. The insurance company then seeks to be recompensed by the defaulting buyer (you!).

When you pay a deposit to secure a pre-construction property, you are guaranteeing that you will proceed with the purchase and finalise the contract once the building is ready. Your deposit is at risk and lost if you do not proceed – in other words, you cannot change your mind.

Conversely, the developer can choose to cancel the contract before it is finalised, enforcing a condition often only in the fine print which gives them the right to do so if they choose. In the Sydney boom of 2011–2015 there were several cases of developers cancelling contracts purely because they knew they could sell the properties at a higher price than for which they were under contract. Legislation was subsequently enacted to prevent this happening again, however in your country it may still be possible. Be sure to carefully check and understand all conditions contained in any contract you sign.

Another situation more common than you may think on such a project is where the developer is unable to continue due to financial pressures, and under these circumstances they can become bankrupt without completion. This can leave you, the buyer, with no property – and you may have waited a long time, passing up other opportunities, for the property to be completed.

When you sign a contract for a property from a developer, you are essentially entering into an agreement with both the developer and the building company it chooses to carry out the work. I have seen many projects that have not been completed because either the developer or the builder has gone into liquidation. If you are buying a development of this type, be sure you ask questions about the builder, such as:

- Which company is it?
- What other projects has it completed?
- Did it complete them within budget?
- Has it planned for cost blowouts?
- What are its financial credentials?

You will want to know the same details about the developer. This information may help protect you from being out of pocket if the venture fails, in that you may not enter into a contract at all if you cannot get satisfactory answers.

ESTABLISHED PROPERTY

When you are considering an established property, you want to be sure that the property is of sound construction and does not have any hidden structural issues or a pest problem. Even property still covered by the builder's warranty may have defects that no-one is aware of. Under those circumstances, you could end up owning a property with significant structural issues which don't come to light until the warranty period has expired, and you will be left bearing the rectification costs.

The most effective way to uncover any defects or the presence of pests is to appoint a pest and/or building inspector to carry out a building inspection. These can usually be done at a reasonable cost (around $500 in Australia) and can be carried out within a day or so of them being requested. Such an inspection should uncover any major structural issues and the presence of common pests, but it may miss some of the smaller defects.

The main problem that you face at this stage is that, even though such inspections are not a major expense, they do cost money. If you have, say, six properties on your list, you don't want to be paying for six inspections only to end up buying just one of the properties. Even if those inspections are tax deductible (and in many countries they are not) you still have to foot the bill and your tax benefit will only be a percentage of that cost.

If you're using these questions the way they are meant to be used, it means that you are most likely to be committed to the process of trusting the data and not needing to travel all over the country to inspect every potential purchase. My book *Investing in the Right Property Now!* covers the important topic of 'growth drivers' and points out that these drivers are less likely to exist where you live than they will in an area which is likely to be further away. To become a savvy and success-ful investor, you can't be travelling all over the country every time you want to buy a property and so you will be using these questions to pick properties without needing to make a visit to personally inspect them.

Even if you do inspect potential properties, few people have the skills needed to be able to pick up on structural issues or detect the presence of pests. Most of us would use such an inspection to form an emotional view of how good the prop-erty is and we would miss any defects. So how do you ensure that the property you buy has no major issues?

The answer is, you can't. You can, however, ensure that if the present owner has any indication at all that there may be a lurking problem, they reveal this to you.

Most countries have some laws around what is known as vendor disclosure. Put simply, this means that before you enter into a contract with a vendor, they must tell you everything they know about the building and any problems. In some countries, *caveat emptor* (let the buyer beware) means that they don't have to tell you these things, and it's up to you to find it out for yourself.

I have found that the best way to reduce the chances of buying a property which subsequently has a major problem is to set out a series of questions in an email and send it to the real estate agent, asking them to have the vendor answer the questions. If you are looking at more than one property the single email can request this information from all of them.

Where the building itself is concerned, you should ask the following questions (a longer list can be found in my book *How to Achieve Property Success*):

- Is there now, or has there ever been, any kind of pest infestation in the property, including (but not limited to) rodents, termites, ants and other insects?

- Has there been any rectification work undertaken in the last 10 years on any part of the building?

- Are there any cracks in the walls or ceilings?

- Is there water ingress, or evidence of past water ingress, into any part of the building?

- Is there any mould present in any part of the building?

- In your opinion, would you attest that this building is structurally sound, and to the best of your knowledge can you exclude any structural issues?

The thing about these questions is that they are pointed, and they are made in writing. Most people might be prepared to withhold information about any defects that they either know of or suspect, but few people will do it in writing. By having these questions answered about all properties which have made your shortlist, you will then have written evidence that may become useful in the future. If you later uncover structural defects which can be proven existed prior to your purchase, you have a stronger case against the vendor to cover the costs of rectification work. It isn't a guarantee that they can be held accountable, but it is one more piece of evidence which may help you in the event of an issue.

RESTRICTED PROPERTY

During your discussions, check that there are no restrictions that may impact negatively on you in the future. For example, if you are buying an older property, there may be heritage-listing issues that may not prevent you from doing renovations but may require you to keep the property in 'good and original' order. This could become an expensive exercise and make even simple renovations far more costly than you hope.

Government may also have particular by-laws that impact on existing housing that you should ask about — for example, a law to prevent additions, or rules about swimming pool fences, facades, driveways, etc. If the property is some form of community, condominium or strata title, you should check the by-laws, rules and covenants for any restrictions on renovations or covenants which prevent certain forms of building or renovation.

NEGOTIATING

The prior questions provided you with a basis on which to commence your negotiations. The information that you discover in this question will provide a further basis for that negotiation.

Once you have narrowed down the price range you should be moving in, and you have taken the temperature of the market, you now need to assess the condition and age of the properties on your list in comparison to other properties which have sold and in comparison to each other.

If you have discovered that there are any defects of the property – small or large – you can then use this information to further discount your offer. You should try to get a vague idea of how much it would cost to rectify any building defects and discount that amount from your offer. Ensure that, when starting your negotiations, you state the discounts you have made and the reason for those discounts.

Just because a building has some issues doesn't mean you should walk away from it. Your capacity to uncover these things and use them as a basis for negotiation could mean that you pick up a bargain which, with the money you subsequently spend on rectification, still comes in at well under market value. The more under market value you can secure a property, the more money you make. Always remember that growth on a property occurs to the market value, not what you paid for the property. If you buy under the market value, you make money straight away, or as soon as that rectification work has been done.

SUMMARY

Unless you are a building inspector or in the building trade, your eyes cannot be trusted to establish whether a property is in good structural condition or not. However, at this stage, which is prior to having an agreed price and contract, you can't spend money on reports and inspection unless you are sure you are going to buy a particular property.

You can go a long way toward extracting information from an agent and a vendor by asking the right questions and being sure you get answers to them in writing. People may withhold the truth from you, but if you ask a direct question *and* get the answer in writing, you are far more likely to uncover any known structural or other negative features of a potential property.

QUESTION SIXTEEN

Is there a rent guarantee or other incentive to buy?

Imagine this: warm golden sun, gentle breezes, swaying palm trees and you, reclining on your sun lounge, drinking margaritas... all made possible by that rent guarantee you received when you bought the latest luxury condo. You probably paid more than it was worth, and the salesperson pocketed enough in commission to finance their own tropical getaway, but that doesn't matter. You have a 10-year rent guarantee – right? Wrong.

I have now been investing in property for almost a quarter of a century and helping people to do the same for just as long. In all of that time, I have never seen a rent guarantee worth the paper it's written on. Why? Because rent guarantees are offered by people and entities, and people and entities go broke, every single day of the week.

A rent guarantee is a promise to pay an agreed sum for an agreed term. It is *not* a promise to get a tenant, nor is it a guarantee that the property can attract the amount of rent specified in the guarantee. The 'guarantor' has no legal obligation to prove that they can actually finance this promise, nor are they required to give any evidence as to how they arrived at the amount of the guarantee.

You will remember the story of Chris, who had purchased a hotel room in a complex that was supposed to be the next best thing. You might think that Chris walked into that arrangement blindly, but in reality, it can be very hard not to believe the marketing hype fed to you by some of these very clever salespeople.

Sadly for Chris, he purchased this property before people had become quite so aware of the dangers. It was the late 1990s and the real estate market was buzzing in the euphoria of an almost 10-year high. The market was overheated and self-pro-claimed property gurus were promising quick riches to many. The bubble had expanded close to bursting point.

Hotel chains saw the chance to realise capital by selling off their real estate while holding on to the business end, the hotel operation, and big names jumped on the bandwagon, carving their buildings up into individually-titled lots or building new property to be sold to hungry investors.

Chris had seen his parents successfully invest in property over a number of years and really wanted to experience similar success. He wanted to be independent and prove that he was capable of fending for himself. As mentioned, he couldn't see much downside, because the 10-year guarantee would allow him to throw cash into his debt, and by the time the guarantee was over, he would be the outright owner.

Poor Chris. When the operators of the hotel (who had offered the rent guarantee) went into liquidation over that failed venture and a number of other mismanaged hotel operations, Chris was left without an income. He went from expecting a cash flow of $4,000 per annum after costs to a shortfall of $9,000 a year just to support the loan. He couldn't let the property, because it didn't even qualify as an apartment, having no kitchen; and, of course, a property with no chance of tenancy is not going to be an attractive option for sale.

A little bit of solid investigation would have led anyone to discover that this particular apartment was never going to deliver. Simple research would have uncovered the following information:

- These types of serviced or vacation apartments are priced according to their expected return, not their market value. This apartment was overpriced.

- There was not sufficient demand for holiday rentals in that area, and there were no plans by the local authorities to add any sort of amenity that would change this fact in the future.

- Hotels in that area already struggled to fill their rooms and had been reporting low occupancy for many years.

- This apartment was not conducive to being used for anything other than hotel accommodation.

- The rent guarantee masked the true potential return of this property and provided false security for the buyers – the economics simply didn't stack up!

Rent guarantees aren't worth the paper they are written on. They cannot magically transform an investment that has other inherent problems. They cannot guarantee that the venture will be managed by experienced and qualified people. They cannot produce tenants where there are none, and they cannot heighten the attractiveness of any property if the market simply does not demand the accommodation.

If a property *needs* a rent guarantee in order to attract buyers, what is wrong with it? Without rental demand and a vibrant economy, all a rent guarantee can ever do is temporarily blind investors to the facts. As far as I am concerned, the only true guarantee that a 'rent guarantee' can give is that you are probably being swindled!

A few years ago I was at a property expo and I spoke in a seminar, quite loudly and robustly, about this very issue. Of course, as it was an expo, the entrance to the seminar room was fringed by exhibitors, many of them offering rent guarantees for the properties they were hawking. After day one, the expo manager took me aside and mentioned that a few exhibitors were upset that I was talking negatively about their strategy, and that they would like me to stop. I told him I wasn't prepared to do that! As far as I was concerned, if the property that these people were selling was good enough, they could ditch the rent guarantees and people would still buy them! Needless to say, I was pretty unpopular for the rest of the weekend – I could almost feel the daggers in my back as I walked the corridors.

I am not suggesting by any means that you should not buy a property that has a rent guarantee. I am, however, suggesting the following:

- A rent guarantee does not remove the need to ask the 20 Must Ask Questions®.

- In some cases, a rent guarantee may be in place because the property would otherwise struggle for tenancy. Be sure to independently confirm true demand for that type of property.

- Rent guarantees are often funded by adding a few thousand dollars to the purchase price. Ask the marketer if you can get a discount if you don't take up the rent guarantee and see what they say. Also, be especially sure that you check that the property is at true market value, so you know you are not paying for that guarantee.

- If the property has otherwise checked out, always confirm the true market rent by checking property search engines. These have rental sections where you can clarify rental returns for properties in many areas. Some of the real estate institute or association websites also provide this service.

GOVERNMENT-GUARANTEED PROPERTY

In some countries, you are able to buy a property which comes with some form of government guarantee. In Australia, the best example is the housing offered by a government-funded company which leases property to the defence forces.

I don't usually use names when I speak for or against anything, but I do not refer to Defence Housing Australia and other such 'government-backed' schemes here with any intention of warning you against them. I mention them because it is important that you know that properties such as these are not 'government-backed' as such, and that having leasing arrangements managed by the government or the defence force will neither add nor take away from a property's attractiveness or security as an investment. If the property goes backward in value, the *government* will *not* refund the capital loss. If the tenant treats the property badly and causes major damage, the *government* will *not* fix that damage for you, although there is some capacity to do some minor cosmetic spruce up at the end of each rental period. The government will pay for repairs and maintenance along the way, but this is covered by a significantly higher than average management fee, up to three times the norm in some states.

So, the answer to the often-asked question, 'What about defence force housing [et al.] – should I buy it?' is, 'I don't know, does it stack up against the 20 Questions?' Any kind of agreement or arrangement post-settlement to manage or otherwise oversee your investment will not be what makes it work for you. It will be the characteristics you uncover when you do your research, the growth drivers and the future potential of the area which will make your property a good investment for you.

If you are offered information about such property, do not be any less diligent in your research. In my experience, the chances of getting a good or a bad property investment are the same with 'government-guaranteed' property as they are with other property. There are no iron-clad guarantees in this world. Nothing can remove the risk you will take each and every time you choose to make an investment of any kind. Minimising it by taking the time to research well is the best risk-management tool you have.

OTHER INCENTIVES

Developers and marketers have been known to offer all manner of incentives to get you to lose sight of the underlying asset, and any potential flaws, and proceed with a property purchase just to obtain that incentive. In the years I have been investing in property I have seen cashbacks, free boats, upgraded appliances, even free holidays offered with the purchase of the property being marketed.

These freebies do not add any value to the property. They cannot turn a poor investment into a good one. Long after the freebies have been used or are forgotten about, you'll be saddled with a property that may not be such a good buy after all. In my experience, if a property is that good, it doesn't need an incentive. If an inducement is being offered, it is a sure sign that the underlying asset is lacking in some way.

EXISTING TENANT

Many investors feel uncomfortable buying a property that doesn't have an existing tenant in place. Equally, some buyers won't buy a property which is owner-occupied rather than leased, as it hasn't demonstrated a demand from tenants.

If you believe that you need an existing tenant in place, on a longer-term lease, consider this: what if you have identified an area currently undergoing pressure on rents? Where rentals are undersupplied, it makes sense that rents will be on the rise. If you have a tenant in place when you buy the property, most countries will require that the tenant be allowed to see out their lease, however long that may be. If rents are rapidly rising during this time, you will have no capacity to increase your rent, and this will be detrimental to you. That long-term lease, which seemed like a security blanket, can quickly become a contract which loses you money.

In order to be sure that you buy a property which will get a tenant, you need to ask these 20 Questions. You particularly need to ensure that your questions about vacancy, demand from tenants and the percentage of the population who do rent are carefully asked and answered. Once you have confirmed these questions, then you don't need a tenant in place before you buy to know that you will get a tenant after the sale has gone through.

TAXATION SCHEMES

In some countries, the provision of certain kinds of housing which may be in short supply may be encouraged by the government by allowing buyers, or builders of such property, to receive special tax treatment. For example, in Australia, the National Rental Affordability Scheme (now defunct) was a failed attempt to provide lower cost rentals for paraprofessional workers, such as nurses and teachers.

The scheme involved generous tax credits for the first 10 years of ownership to anyone willing to buy such a property and rent it to the appropriate target groups for 20 per cent under market rent. Larger developers flocked to the scheme, building houses, villas and apartments in their hundreds, then on-selling them – along with the available tax credits – to individual investors.

The issues were many but mainly related to the fact that all the scheme did was open doors for more dodgy spruikers to take advantage of investors and sell more property. Developments occurred in areas with few of the fundamentals that these 20 Questions cover, and by way of the tax credit scheme, which seemed like free money, the properties were easily sold to people who were buying for the tax benefits alone, without checking out whether there were any other redeeming qualities of the properties themselves.

What we saw happen was that, as hundreds of these properties flooded markets with low demand, oversupply forced prices *and* rents down. Buyers quickly found themselves with properties worth up to $100,000 less than they had paid. With market rent plummeting and the requirement to offer property at 20 per cent below that level, cash flows for the investors were extremely negative. The generous yearly tax credit didn't come close to making up for the value and cash flow loss, and a raft of unhappy investors were left with property they couldn't sell. The developers, and their middlemen marketers, walked away pocketing handsome profits and exorbitant sales commissions, without looking back.

The lesson is this: Where there is a tax or other financial incentive offered which looks too good to be true, it more than likely is. Your research must be impeccable, and you must confirm that the property being offered would be property that you would buy if there was no incentive on offer.

SUMMARY

Stay away from properties where there is a rent guarantee or other incentive unless you can absolutely confirm that the 20 Questions are well satisfied and the area itself has merit. Incentives and guarantees are usually only offered when the developer is having trouble with sales, and they are a sign to you that the underlying property asset is likely to have few redeeming features.

You are close to the end of your research – there are just a few more things which need clarification. Read on to Question Seventeen.

QUESTION SEVENTEEN

What will the property management arrangement be?

You may think that having your property managed is something you don't need to worry about until the ink is dry on the contract and you are ready to find a tenant. However, this isn't true, because knowing the various types of property management that may be available before you go too far with property selection is vital. This is because there is a variety of possible management arrangements for all types of property, and knowing which is most suited for the property you have narrowed down to will prevent you travelling a path towards buying a property for which the subsequent management arrangements are not to your liking. There are so many variations on standard management these days that it is worth devoting an entire question to it.

A complete discussion about property management, its costs, and interviewing and recruiting a property manager is contained in one of the chapters of *How to Achieve Property Success*. It's a great chapter to read because it will help you to reduce the chances that you will end up with a manager who does little other than diminish the value of your asset through poor management.

In this question I will review the subject in slightly less detail, simply to assist you to come to some conclusions about what you will and won't be prepared to accept. Later, when you are ready to select actual properties, you would be well advised to become better informed about property management.

RESIDENTIAL PROPERTY ON LONGER-TERM LEASES

If you purchase a house, apartment or villa that will attract tenancy of a longer-term nature (that is, in excess of six months, and up to several years), you can do one of two things: self-manage or retain a professional property management company to manage for you.

Many property investors feel they would rather opt for self-management. Stated reasons for this include that they would like to 'keep an eye' on the property, or they wish to save money on management costs. I believe that if such investors understood what was involved in the daily management of a rental property, they wouldn't think this way. Many investors who start out managing their own property quickly decide that it is far better to have a professional do it for them.

Self-managing your property means that the process of selecting tenants, collecting rent, arranging maintenance and supervising the lease period falls to you. You must collect and manage rental bonds and arrange for them to be lodged in a trust account. You need to be on call day and night to respond to demands from tenants and attend to urgent repairs and maintenance. And you do all this to save the tax-deductible cost of a property manager, which is likely to be a small fraction of the rent collected, and well worth not having to do these jobs yourself!

Most investors find that the after-tax cost of professional management is money well spent to avoid these tasks. Professional managers have access to bad tenant databases and the skill to choose suitable tenants. They have economies of scale which allow them to access tradespeople, manage rents via professional systems, and collect and remit rent to you regularly. And it is *they* who must be on call to manage those middle-of-the-night urgent repairs.

These days, there are several options when choosing a professional manager. For example, you can select a property manager linked to a real estate agency, or you can use the services of a company that exists only for property management. Usually a company that is independent of a real estate agency will employ professionals trained in property management; a company attached to a real estate agency is more likely to employ and train in-house. This is not always the case, however, and once you have chosen and settled on a property, you will need to undertake a fairly lengthy process to choose the right manager.

Once a manager is chosen, you sign an agreement – which is a contract between you and the manager – retaining them to provide management services for the property in question. These contracts are legally binding and many of them have unacceptable clauses, such as long termination periods if you are unhappy with their performance, or unreasonable charges for inspections. In addition, management agreements are governed by the laws of the state and country and, in many countries, each state has a different law, and thus a different type of agreement. Reading the agreements in full and deleting, changing or adding any clauses you wish is important. Many new landlords simply sign what is sent to them, unaware that this contract is as negotiable as any other. Again, I caution you to become familiar with property management first. Find out as much information as you can yourself or read one of my other books.

OTHER MANAGEMENT POSSIBILITIES

If you have purchased a standard residential property, it is likely that management will be as per the previous section. If the property is going to be available for short-term or holiday (vacation) lease, the agreement will be in essence the same, with some small differences. The most notable difference will be a higher management fee to compensate the manager for the shorter periods of tenancy and the higher turnover of tenants. If you are thinking of purchasing any other kind of property, it may well come under a very different management structure, such as a professional management agreement, management rights or a leaseback.

On-site management agreement

An on-site management agreement is typically a contract between an owners' (or condominium) corporation (body corporate) and a manager who is retained to provide on-site caretaking and management services in a complex generally rented for holiday periods and short-term leases. This agreement can take many forms and is essentially designed by the body corporate. It will contain strict termination requirements to prevent a situation where a manager devotes their entire life (and possibly that of their family) to the job, and subsequently finds themselves out on the street.

The agreement also outlines how the manager will be paid. Usually the fee for management is a set amount, which will be higher than standard fees as it covers more activity. However, sometimes only a maximum fee is set and the on-site manager is expected also to manage the property financially, distributing only net income to the owners after meeting all required costs.

In addition, the agreement will cover how the manager and body corporate intend to work together and the duties required of the manager, which include but are not limited to:

- providing letting services – booking individual apartments to holiday-makers

- advertising and marketing

- on-site repairs and maintenance
- arranging tours
- collecting tariffs.

When you buy a property that has an on-site management arrangement, you may not be able to remove your individual apartment from the agreement. So, if you are unhappy with the management while others are happy, you will be outvoted. If properties with this kind of arrangement are on your list for consideration, be sure to ask ahead of time for a copy of the management agreement, so that you can ensure that you are thoroughly familiar with its contents.

Management rights

Management rights are unique to Australia, although other countries have forms of this kind of agreement. Similar to a professional management agreement, they usually include equity in the property in some form. Typically, a management rights agreement grants the manager ownership of the reception area and offices and any café, bar, restaurant or pool and spa area. This means that it becomes difficult to terminate a poorly performing manager, as essentially they must be able to on-sell this equity to a party whom the body corporate accepts.

While management agreements are more common for holiday (vacation) apartments, management rights are common in larger hotels. This is because these hotels were usually initially owned by the hotel operators who subsequently sold the rooms to investors but retained the ownership of the remaining property.

Management rights are extremely complex and you, as an owner, will have very minimal rights. Often the management fees are incredibly high: this is the reason owners do not get as great a share in the profits as they might have hoped. Further, it is usually not possible to withdraw your apartment from a management rights agreement, since the common areas are owned by the manager. I recommend against buying property with these kinds of agreements in place. If you are considering such a property, ensure that a lawyer looks over the agreement before you sign any purchase contracts.

Leasebacks

A leaseback is a contract between you and an on-site manager that assigns the manager the right to let out your property, receive rental payments and arrange and supervise maintenance. Unlike a management agreement or management rights, a leaseback is an individual contract with each owner, and so it is much easier to rescind or not renew. It is like a combination of a management agreement and a lease (a contract between the property manager and the tenant).

The intent of a leaseback is for the manager to become your tenant. How they subsequently use your property is outlined in the agreement – they may agree to on-let it on a weekly, monthly or nightly basis. Since the lease is between you and the manager, it means that you have a tenant for the term of that lease. If the property subsequently suffers vacancy, that is a problem for the manager, and they must continue to pay the agreed rent to you regardless.

A leaseback is most likely to be offered in a situation where you could otherwise use your property in any way you wished – to live in it yourself or lease it independently. They are rarely offered where all of the properties in a complex are needed to make a venture viable, although this does occur.

Self-management for vacation letting

These days, self-managing your vacation or holiday property has become much easier through the use of online sites such as Airbnb, Vrbo.com and many other similar websites. These sites allow you to choose the length of the occupancy and give you a lot of flexibility around availability, pricing and the offer.

While these sites give you flexibility and control, it is important to understand that they are simply booking sites, and no other management services are offered. Just as with a standard residential property, all of the responsibilities of management, including having in place the correct insurances and local government permission, falls to you as the owner.

Before making this decision, I urge you to read the section in *How to Achieve Property Success* which outlines the benefits and drawbacks of this decision. It is my own personal experience that the drawbacks far outweigh any perceived benefits of self-management on any property.

RIGHTS AND RESPONSIBILITIES

Although you have yet to choose a property, it is useful at this stage to point out that every state of Australia and every country in the world has its own residential tenancy laws. These laws assign rights and responsibilities to both the landlord and the tenant, and failure as a landlord to fulfil your rights can result in severe financial penalties and, in extreme (and thankfully rare) cases, prison time.

Access to information about these rights and responsibilities can be found on the website of the government department responsible for residential tenancy laws in your country. Once you have narrowed down your search for property to a single state, it may be worthwhile to download a copy of the appropriate law and become familiar with it.

SUMMARY

There are many forms of property management and, depending on the property type, the management available on something you are looking at may well be something you are unfamiliar with.

Once you have bought a property, the successful ongoing management of it will be critical to keeping your asset in good order. This isn't something that you can treat lightly, so be sure you fully understand the management, and don't try to do it yourself.

Always remember that you are reading this book to become a property *investor* and not a property manager. Trying to be both may mean that you are successful with neither.

Now, let's move on to Question Eighteen.

QUESTION EIGHTEEN

Is the property suitable for the demographics and what condition is it in?

As you approach the final stages of your research, it is likely that you now have on your list the properties on which you will be making an offer. It's rare to get this far with a big list of property and then find, once you ask these final questions, that none of them suit you after all. You most certainly will have at least narrowed down the areas in which you are looking to make that choice, and you should have a shortlist of properties from which you have eliminated those which may have significant structural issues or don't suit you for other reasons that you have uncovered.

As it is more than likely that you will be looking for property from the comfort of your own home or office, the next few questions specifically examine properties in such a way that you can refine your ability to choose the right property without needing to inspect it.

I still recall a time when I was speaking at a function and outlining the process I use to buy a property without needing to travel all over the country eyeballing all of my options. At the end of the speech, a woman approached me and told me that she didn't have any idea how I could possibly buy a property sight unseen. 'What if it has structural problems?', she asked. 'What if it has? How would I be able to tell?', was my response. I guess the point is that, if I go to look at a property to buy, I am only going to be involving myself in the emotional aspects of that property. I am going to buy it because I like it, not because it is necessarily a good investment. Once I have seen it, it becomes much harder for me to maintain my objectivity and do my research well.

Just because *I* don't view the property, it doesn't mean that I don't retain others to do so for me. The chances of me buying a structurally unsound or badly maintained dud are limited by the things that I do after I have made my selection, and before I enter into a contract. I am incredibly careful when it comes to selection of a property – I just don't go along and see it for myself.

IS THIS PROPERTY THE RIGHT TYPE?

In earlier questions we have examined areas in terms of who lives there, for the purposes of determining if they are a target group that can assist in driving growth. Areas with ageing populations rarely result in significant growth, and in areas with a family demographic demand is likely to exceed supply, where all other questions are also satisfied.

In Question Four we examined demographics and talked about how important it is to know who lives in an area so that you can choose the right property *type*. It is at this stage that you must make sure that the property types on your list are appropriate for the area demographics.

In areas where young, upwardly mobile couples reside, apartments with amenities very close by will be in demand. Usually, the better choice of property will be in areas close to public transport. The kinds of facilities demanded by this group will also need to be nearby – such as 24-hour gyms and convenience stores.

Where the demographics are young couples with pre-school children, the preferred property type is often a villa or townhouse, with some backyard and access to pre-schools, childcare centres and community centres.

Areas with a predominance of families with older children will need freestanding houses with backyards. It will be important to choose a property with the number of bedrooms most consistent with the demand from the particular family demographic in that area. Check out the sales figures and find out what size of property has the highest sales numbers.

Populations of 'downsizers', for whom the kids have left school, will be looking for a smaller number of bedrooms, easy care yards and access to cultural amenities and other appropriate services. Many will prefer low-set dwellings to high-rise.

Go down your list and check that you have selected property types which are appropriate rather than just those that seem like good value. You might want to get into the market more easily by buying a cheaper or smaller apartment or house, but if that property type isn't right for the demographics, it will be a false economy that will not pay off over the longer term.

THE AGE OF THE PROPERTY

While the actual age of a property is not always apparent when you are looking at it, and the selling agent won't always provide this detail, it is important to you for two reasons. The first reason is that the older a property, the more funds you must allow for potential repair costs when you are performing your initial calculations.

I recall a time when in my own investment portfolio I had a sudden breakdown of a whole raft of hot water heaters. My portfolio contains a mix of old and newer properties, and some of them are considerably old. I was pretty happy with the fact that I hadn't experienced much in the way of repairs, major or minor, and so in the back of my mind I expected *something* to happen sometime soon.

At the beginning of that year, I got a call from one of my property managers telling me that a new hot water heater was required in one of the properties which I had only acquired the prior year – bad luck but it can happen; two weeks later I received a call from the manager of another property with the same request. Within six months I had received eight similar calls! I remember feeling like I wanted to cry when I got call number seven, but laughing like mad when I got the eighth call. The poor manager making that eighth call had no idea what was so funny, and she told me that it was, for her, a rare reaction to get from a landlord! My PA had to remind me that I had been pretty lucky to date, and that in the grand scheme of things it was not as bad as it seemed.

If you buy an older property, you will be called upon to provide funds for maintenance. In order to cater for this, you should be negotiating a discount to the purchase price. My advice is to ask the vendor, prior to making an offer, to provide facts such as the age of the hot water heater and air conditioners, whether taps and sinks have been upgraded and the condition of the window treatments. Ask to see photos of these specific things. That way, when you negotiate you can say things like, 'I am making this low offer because I am anticipating that I will need to replace the hot water heater and the air conditioner soon after settlement.'

The second reason for establishing the age of the property is because, in countries where depreciation claims are part of your tax allowances, the time frame over which you can make claims for capital works deductions (that is, the loss in value of the actual building) can depend on the original construction date and the type of the building. In addition to discovering if you can make depreciation claims, you will want to know the time frame over which you can continue to make claims, as this will most definitely affect your cash flows.

Remember, the property that you are going to buy does not have to have depreciation claims available for it to be a suitable purchase. Depreciation claims do, however, add to your cash flows and make it easier to achieve a positive cash flow in the early years when you need them most. Later, as the debt and your expenses reduce and your rents increase with inflation and market demand, your property will be able to maintain itself without needing the tax refund which can result in a claim for depreciation. This means that a property with shorter available terms of depreciation (or none at all) may be suitable, as long as you are aware of the need to work on the debt and increase rents when you can.

To find out the age of a property, ask the agent selling the property. If they don't know, ask them to find out. You can also call the local government – it should have the original development application on file and be able to quote an original contract date. Barring that, there are a number of websites that provide free property data, and all you need to do is Google the property address to find those sites which have the most comprehensive data and the original construction dates.

THE CONDITION OF THE PROPERTY

In Question Fifteen, you attempted to establish whether there may potentially be any major structural issues with properties on your list. Once you have negotiated an agreed price on a property, and before you enter into an unconditional contract to buy it, you should have a pest and building inspection done. Some companies offer both together and other companies do one or the other. The cost of such an inspection is variable, depending upon how thorough they are. In Australia, it is usually somewhere around $500. Be careful of cut-price pest and building inspections – they usually operate according to a simple check-box approach and rarely examine the substructure or the roof spaces. This isn't the time to cut costs and try to get a budget inspection done.

It is likely that at some time in your property journey (and probably more than once) you will pay for a pest and building inspection to be completed and, as a result of that report, decide not to proceed with the purchase. You must consider this a cost of investing and, if you invest well, this cost will become insignificant. Most importantly, don't feel you must go ahead with a purchase in the face of a bad report just because you paid out the money to have it prepared!

As well as knowing more about the structural integrity of the building, you need to know whether or not the property is habitable. The areas of most concern are:

- the condition of the major plant and equipment in the building, such as hot water heaters and taps
- the condition of the paintwork and window treatments
- the age and condition of floor coverings and light fittings
- the potential for the property to be leased immediately, and what needs to be done before it can be let.

All of these things relate to your immediate ability to get an income, and they help you to determine the costs that you may face upon settlement of your new investment. This will help you to plan better. You can also use the potential cost of any minor renovations in the negotiation phase as a way of getting further discounts. This information will assist you in determining whether your new property will be immediately available to rent out or if you may have to wait and do some work on it before it's ready for its first tenant. It will also help you to plan your cash flows in those early weeks.

Ask the agent

While the agent is most definitely working for the vendor, and by law must keep the best interest of the vendor at heart, they also must answer any direct questions you pose to the best of their ability. Since that is the case, you should ask:

- Are you able to ascertain the approximate age of the hot water heater?

- Are there any minor issues that you think need to be attended to – for example, leaky or loose taps, creaky or wobbly doors, worn or broken fixtures and fittings?

- How long before curtains, blinds and floor coverings will need replacing?

- Are there any loose tiles or kitchen and bathroom benches needing repair?

- Are all appliances in good working order?

- If you owned this property, is there anything you would do before you leased it? Would you repaint, change the window treatments, and so on?

Agents are obliged by law to answer specific questions with the truth as they know it. Don't be afraid to ask them to go and ask the vendor. Make notes about the conversation and ensure that the agent knows you are keeping this record. This way, if any of the information given to you later proves to have been misleading, you have some evidence with which to seek recompense.

Call a local property manager

The condition of the property relates to whether or not things are in good working order or need replacement sometime soon. It also relates to whether pests are present and whether the structure is sound.

The ability of a property to attract, and retain, a tenant depends upon these things, but also upon the actual presentation of a property. While you don't need to be buying property with all the bells and whistles, with features that are likely to attract a higher price but not more rent, you do need to be sure that the property is in a condition which means that there is little, or nothing, to do for a tenant to move straight in as soon as the purchase is finalised. Since I have advised you that you shouldn't be traipsing all over the country inspecting properties and racking up a large, possibly non-deductible travel bill, let me share a little trick I have been using to ensure that someone with experience in these things takes a look at the property *before* I have made that final offer to buy.

Regardless of whether the property is currently managed or not, call an *alternative* local property manager to the manager who may be attached to the selling agent, tell them you are considering this purchase and ask them to inspect the property. Ideally, you want them to be able to enter the property, and you would have to ask the selling agent for permission for this. If you are not comfortable doing this, or are unable to make these arrangements, at least ask the manager if they can provide a general idea of how rentable the property is.

Ask them to look at the exterior and interior and comment on presentation. Ask them to consider the area in which it is situated, too, and if, in their opinion, this area will be in demand by tenants. This manager can uncover undesirable aspects such as poor location, a possible bad neighbourhood or any other apparent drawbacks even from the outside. In the event that they can do an internal inspection, ask them to check on all the things you previously asked the selling agent.

A good manager will happily carry out this work for you in an effort to eventually obtain your agreement for them to manage this property. If you find a manager who will, award them the management contract – clearly they are willing to go outside the square to get business.

Once you have found out all of the above details, you will be as informed as you would have been had you inspected the property yourself, without the related emotional attachment. You will be able to use this information to keep the property on your list, or to delete it at this point.

Other things affecting condition

Most properties will be in residential areas where you can expect that there will be no negative impact to affect your continued letting and profiting from its growth when it becomes your investment.

From time to time, though, properties are situated in areas that may be subject to some form of impediment of which you, or the present owner, may be unaware. For example, the area that you are looking at may:

- be exposed to mine subsidence

- be situated in a 'one in one hundred years' (or more often) flood zone, or be on a flood plain

- have had past exposure to a ground or water contaminant of some kind

- be on a fault line and potentially exposed to earthquake

- be at risk of landslip

- have been built on reclaimed land which could, at some time in the future, be unstable.

This list is by no means exhaustive and any number of potential impediments could negatively affect you in the future, and not only cost you money for rectification, but leave you with a property you cannot rent out which also loses value. In some of the worst cases, class action lawsuits ensue which can take years to settle, and still not settle in any satisfactory matter.

While some of these things cannot be determined ahead of time, and any known impacts on land you are about to buy are usually required to be disclosed in purchase contracts, being aware that these things can exist may help you to ask the right questions about an area, and property, that you are looking at.

SUMMARY

While pest and building inspections will uncover pest and structural problems, you also need to know that the property is in a condition that will allow it to be rented without delay. Many of the smaller items covered in this question may prevent this from occurring. Be sure you get the vendor to attend to as many of these things as possible by asking them to fix them as part of your agreement. If you can't do this, be sure to achieve a reduction in price to cover your costs of bringing the property up to a habitable condition.

The next thing to consider, once you are satisfied with the condition of a property, is whether it is appropriate for the relevant tenant demographic. This is covered in Question Nineteen.

QUESTION NINETEEN

Is the property tenant-appropriate?

One of the messages you will have been receiving loud and clear since you first began to read this book is that, to be a successful property investor, it is critical that you remain unemotional. I have warned you against looking at property in person, to ensure that your own personal feelings and opinions (which are not valid in this case) don't impede upon you making the right choices. I have given you a huge amount of information so that you don't have to take a single step outside your home or office to buy a perfectly acceptable property with the greatest chance of investing success.

And now I am asking you, 'Is it tenant-appropriate?' It would seem that the only way you can answer that question would be to jump on a plane or in a car and take a good long look at the property, to check out whether the taps are right and there is no expensive timber flooring just waiting to be damaged.

However, it certainly is not. You can find this out in exactly the same way as you have found out all of your information up to this point – by using other eyes and by asking pointed questions.

Think for a moment about your own home. You have worked pretty hard to make it feel just right, for you. Over the years you have made it into your castle, buying accessories and decorating it *your* way. If you put it on the market today, you might take the time to fix up any little problems, change the taps, paint a few walls, and so on. However, you feel comfortable in it, and to the best of your ability you most likely have filled it with nice little touches that make it not just a home, but something you are proud of.

Imagine that you needed to go away for six months. How would you feel about renting out your property? Would you worry about anything? Is your property designed to withstand treatment by someone not as careful as you, someone who does not have the vested interest of an owner? The property you buy to rent out ultimately should not suit you – it should suit the tenant. All the things that you look for in a home are probably the very things you do *not* want in the property you rent out! Making sure the property is tenant-friendly may protect you both emotionally and financially.

THE PROPERTY IN GENERAL

When you let out your property, you – most likely via your property manager – will be doing your best to get a good tenant. Your property manager will search tenant databases to be sure there are no black marks against that tenant and, to the best of their ability, choose someone who will care for the property.

The realities are, though, that not all tenants will treat your property as they would their own. Therefore, the interior of any property you consider buying must be able to withstand a degree of lack of care by the occupants. While tenants do have a legal obligation to care for your property, you cannot reasonably expect them to live as meticulously as you may do yourself, and to have as much respect for things they do not own. Rather than cry your eyes out when a tenant leaves your property looking the worse for wear, you can prevent the issue altogether by being sure that a property starts out being suitable to let.

The following elements are a good idea:

- Make sure that the property you choose has floor coverings that do not require too much care. I personally like tiles or vinyl and have been known to tear up old carpet and replace it with floor coverings that are more easy care. These days you can purchase wood-floor-style vinyls that are inexpensive to both buy and lay. If the carpets are neutral-coloured and plush, be prepared for them to look awful in a few months and need a solid yearly clean.

- Have fixtures of a medium to low standard. Brass tap fittings will go green, and high-quality light fittings and so on may not be cared for. Basic fixtures and fittings can easily be replaced from the local large hardware chain at a fraction of the cost of more expensive items.

- Have neutral decor, with one colour throughout. It is much easier to let out a property with neutral decor, and cheaper to repaint. Fancy paintwork needs maintenance and only looks good when it is new.

- The exterior of the property should be very low maintenance and have as little garden as possible, unless the cash flows make it possible for you to hire a gardener. Most tenants will not care for gardens. In all of our many properties, I think we have only one tenant who gardens! The ideal yard will have ample paving. Where there is grass, you may need to pay for mowing if you want this done regularly.

- Pools – note that these are a *bad* idea, unless you are going to pay for chemicals and ask the tenant to be sure it is regularly cleaned. I have found that pools don't add a lot of rent, and in many cases they can be a detriment to families – and remember, families are the target group most likely to impact on growth!

I personally like a property to be constructed of brick (inside and out), have tiled floors with vertical blinds, no air conditioner and no gardens. Those are the tenant-friendly properties that give me the least amount of grief, unless they have students in them. That's another story!

THE FURNITURE

Some people are sold property that is fully furnished, the theory being that furniture will bring a higher-rental return and provide more on-paper deductions, creating higher cash flows. This might be true in isolated cases, but generally a furnished property is harder to let than an unfurnished one – unless, of course, the property targets either a holiday (vacation) market or tenants who are very itinerant.

You most probably should steer away from a furnished property, as it will be harder to let. Some years ago we tried to let out a furnished property in Neutral Bay in Sydney. We even priced the rent at the same level as an unfurnished property, and still couldn't get a tenant! In the end we found a tenant but had to take the furniture out, at the cost of three weeks' rent to hire a removalist. Our property definitely was not tenant-friendly until we moved the furniture (which we stored in our garage for many years!).

THE EXTRAS

Air conditioners may attract tenants to your property in tropical North Queensland, but all they will do to a property in Tasmania is cost you a yearly service fee. As mentioned in a prior section, a pool might attract a newly married couple but will probably keep away families with young children. That might suit you, but if families is the group you have identified as having the most demand for your property, it will be a problem.

Consider the cost and the benefits of some of these extras in the property you are considering. The expense of chlorinating that pool and servicing that air conditioner will come straight from your cash flows. Be sure that you can get an equivalent rent increase before going ahead with a property that has any of these expensive extras.

LANDLORD'S INSURANCE

Holding landlord's insurance will not make a property more tenant-friendly, but it may help you in the event that anything in your property is damaged by your tenants. As you would expect, not all policies are the same, and you should shop around. You will want your policy to cover these items:

- Building and contents – where the property is strata or community titled, you will need 'gap' cover, as your body or condominium corporate insurance may only cover items of a common property nature. It will not cover you for damage to, say, an internal wall, and nor will your contents insurance, since it is a building matter. Be sure to check this out.

- Malicious damage caused by tenants.

- Loss of rent because a tenant has left owing money, or because the property is uninhabitable due to tenant damage.

- The legal costs of pursuing a tenant through the court system.

- Public liability – in my other books, I have discussed trusts obtained for property protection purposes and explained why I believe they are not needed. If the tenant sues you because they hurt themselves, the action is covered by public liability, usually up to $10 million or more – and in Australia we have a cap on claims to ensure that any lawsuit against you does not blow out to ridiculous amounts. Check on the situation in your country, though, as some countries are far more litigious than laid-back Australia!

Before you make an offer on a property, call the major insurance companies to ensure there are no exclusions on the area or on the property type you are selecting. You do not want to buy a property and then find that you cannot insure it fully. In addition, you want to check:

- the excess on the policy for each claim
- the maximum number of weeks' rental loss the policy will pay
- the maximum claim amount in any one claim
- the weekly cost of the policy.

Be very careful – some property managers offer a low-cost insurance policy, the premiums of which are deducted from your collected rent automatically. My experience with these policies is that they do not offer as comprehensive a cover as independent policies that may only cost a few dollars more. You must do a complete analysis on any policy you are considering.

WEAR AND TEAR

Even if you have a low-maintenance property, there will be an amount of wear and tear on the property throughout each tenancy. Just as in your own home, things wear out with use over time, and it has to be expected that everything will at some time need replacing, depending upon how long you hold the property for. This is why some countries allow for deprecation as a tax deduction.

You must have a realistic expectation of the wear and tear which is likely to affect your property over the normal course of a tenancy. Landlord's insurance won't cover normal wear and tear and you cannot withhold any bond or deposit paid at the beginning of a tenancy to fix this wear and tear. You need to expect it and plan for it, by ensuring that you put aside funds along the way to deal with it when it occurs.

SUMMARY

You have gone to a lot of trouble to be sure you understand the types of people living in an area. Now is the time to not only be sure that the property type you are buying is suitable for that demographic, but that the property itself is in a condition and style which suits tenanting over the long term. Remember, you are not going to live there yourself, so high-end styling and expensive fixtures and fittings are most likely not necessary.

Also, don't forget landlord's insurance. It is crucial, not negotiable and should be considered a cost of investing.

Now you're ready for Question Twenty.

QUESTION TWENTY

What are the title arrangements?

We have finally arrived at the final question and there is one last major job to attend to – uncovering information about the title arrangements for the property. While you have not selected a property just yet, you will have a fair idea of the type of property that the demographics in the area demand. You probably know whether you are looking for a house, an apartment or something a little more niche market. It is important that you understand the responsibilities of each type of property title and their ramifications for you as an investor.

Title arrangements vary from country to country, and if you are not Australian based, you should be sure you are familiar with the title arrangements in your own country. Note that, although property title arrangements in Australia are a state-based area of law, and they vary in all countries, in the main titles are similar from state to state and country to country.

FREEHOLD TITLE

Known in Australia as Torrens Title (or Green Title in Western Australia), a freehold title is the most common form of title and gives the owner a guarantee of a clear title. This means that once you buy the property you can be sure no-one can come along and claim that the title is not yours!

A freehold title will generally include everything inside the boundaries of the land, but sometimes there are 'easements' – these are rights of way for authorities such as the electricity and water boards, which allow them to run pipes or cables through your property if needed. You are not legally allowed to refuse access to these easements.

Since a freehold title shares no common property, you do not have any kind of levies to pay to other people. You will, however, have to pay rates on the market value of the land, and if you have passed the tax-free threshold on the land value in the area in which you are buying, you may also incur land tax in countries where this applies.

STRATA TITLE (CONDOMINIUM)

Serviced apartments and properties in a block of apartments, villas, a seniors' accommodation complex (retirement community) or a hotel or resort will have a title which allows for the space within the four walls of each individual property to be owned by the owner, according to the laws about that title in the country you are buying. In Australia, these titles can be known as strata titles, and in the US they are more commonly called condominium titles.

Your strata or condominium title may include the title to car-parking arrangements and possibly a storage area. These titles are created in recognition of the fact that some areas will be common to everyone and funds may be needed for upkeep. By law, an owners' corporation, or body corporate or condominium corporation, must be formed and every owner given membership.

The body corporate's office bearers are elected, and usually comprise a chair, a secretary and a treasurer to keep the books balanced. A levy is collected from each owner for the maintenance of the common areas. This levy most often has two parts: an administration levy, which pays for the everyday upkeep of the common areas, and a capital works fund, which allows money to be saved towards eventual upgrading of major items such as roofs, pathways or pools. The amount of your contribution depends on the size of your apartment, rather than on how long you have owned it.

If you are buying a property that has a strata, condominium or some form of community title (see below), you have extra due diligence work to do. Make sure that the capital works fund has a healthy balance. The older the property, the more money will be needed in this fund. It is not unheard of to buy a property and six months later be asked to contribute a large sum to fund major works that the capital works fund cannot cover.

To examine the corporate records, you have to ask your conveyancer or legal representative to carry out a special owners' corporation search. The cost of such a search in Australia is around $300. You will want to know how much your contribution to the various funds will be, and the total value of the quarterly contributions. Some properties have gyms, pools, tennis courts and barbecue areas, and consequently have high owners' corporation fees. These high fees will impact your cash flows if you have not anticipated them.

Owners' corporation fees are usually considered a cost of earning an income and are therefore tax-deductible, but you only get back a percentage equal to your personal marginal rate of tax.

COMPANY TITLE

In rare cases in Australia, the original building is owned under a company title. Under this arrangement, you do not own a property title at all. Instead, you own shares in the company that owns the property. Usually there will be some sort of levy to pay, as there is common property to maintain. Company title is not overly common, but still does exist. Banks usually will not lend to you for such a purchase, as they cannot take a mortgage over the property, since there is no title to receive.

COMMUNITY TITLE

Community title has only been in existence since 1989 in Australia, and it is similar to a strata or condominium title. The difference is that a community title is commonly applied to a major land subdivision where shared areas are provided for the enjoyment of the homeowners.

The homeowners still have title to their own homes, which are usually freestanding houses, but they also have use of playgrounds, parks and so on. There is no common property as in a strata title, but there is shared property, and so a levy of some description will usually be raised.

LESS COMMON TYPES OF TITLE

In each state and country, you may come across rare or obsolete types of title you have never heard of before such as 'leasehold', 'pastoral title' or 'native title'. I have yet to come across any of these while purchasing any of my own properties, and have not found anyone else who has either. In the event that you do, call your lawyer or conveyancer for advice before proceeding.

TITLE INSURANCE

In many countries where property investing is popular, you are able to obtain title insurance. Title insurance protects you against legal risks that can threaten the ownership of your property or affect your right to occupy and use your land. These risks include:

- illegal building works
- boundary issues
- fraud and forgery against your certificate of title
- unpaid rates and taxes

- unregistered rights of way and easements
- adverse possession
- zoning non-compliance.

If you feel more comfortable dotting all of your i's and crossing all of your t's, this may be an insurance you would like to obtain. I have never used it and have never found any detriment in any property I have bought because I am thorough with the questions that I ask. It's for you to consider whether you need this kind of insurance and, if you think you do, ask your legal representative to arrange it for you.

IN WHOSE NAME?

In other books I explore the important question of in whose name you should buy property. For a full discussion of why this is important, be sure to read *How to Achieve Property Success*.

If you are investing alone, then you just need to decide whether you will invest in your own name, or in the name of a trust or company. Investing in your own name has the highest tax advantages and a company or trust structure can remove some of those good benefits, especially in the early years. If you aren't sure which entity to choose, you need to have a conversation with your accountant. This conversation needs to consider not only how you would like things to look at the end of your property investing life, but also what is most beneficial now, when you likely need your tax benefits more.

Where you are investing with a partner, the question becomes more complicated again because you have to consider who needs the tax benefits most now and who will need them later. You can invest either as joint tenants or as tenants in common, and each has its own benefits and drawbacks.

Once you have signed a contract, you cannot make changes to the way the titles are assigned, at least not without incurring considerable costs which may even include double stamp duties or taxes if they are applicable. You can't afford to get this part wrong, so as you reach the end of these questions be sure to have a discussion with a qualified tax adviser about what is the best structure for you.

———

This might seem like an unimportant question, but knowing the title arrangements of a property before you proceed is paramount, as it will give you a list of questions to ask the selling agent – questions such as:

- Are there any outstanding fencing disputes with neighbours?

- Do you know of any easements on the property?

- What are the owners' corporation levies/community title/condominium title contributions?

- In what condition are the common areas?

- Are there any current disputes within the owners' corporation?

- Is this freehold title able to be subdivided? (Ask this in the event that you have found a large block that you may consider developing in the future.)

- Can I make this a dual-occupancy residence (that is, add a second dwelling without subdividing)?

- Are there any current covenants on this title (that is, restrictions on what can be built, what colour you can paint the roof, and so on)?

- Are there any caveats (restrictions on sale) on this title?

Again, the real estate agent may not know the answers to all these questions, so email a list and ask them to get back to you in a day or so with their replies.

SUMMARY

You must have a sound understanding of what each property can offer you in terms of its title arrangements, as well as knowing how you are going to structure that title, and in whose name(s) you will buy.

You are now very close to being ready to go back to Question One and perform your cash flow calculations in more detail on the properties that have made it all the way to this last question. There is, however, one more very important question that you simply cannot miss. Read on.

BONUS QUESTION
Are you being commercial in your approach?

Wait. Isn't this book called the 20 Must Ask Questions®? Why are there 21 questions? Let me explain with a story of why I simply had to include a bonus question in this updated and revised edition of my bestselling book.

A number of years ago, I was in Adelaide running a seminar. Just before this, we had purchased a couple of properties in the northern suburbs of Adelaide, sight unseen. I landed early and had several hours to kill, so I called my husband and told him I was going to hire a car and drive out to look at the properties. 'Don't do that,' he warned, 'You are not going to like them!'

Since I had done a good degree of due diligence prior to buying, I knew that everything would be okay, and besides, many of our clients were starting to buy in the same area. I felt it my duty to look at it with my own eyes. So I called the property manager, made arrangements to meet him at the property, and away I went.

I pulled up, took one look at the duplex we owned, then phoned my husband again and said, 'We're slum lords!' As I entered the property, my sinking feeling sunk even further, and I wondered what had possessed me to buy such a property.

Once we were done and standing by the roadside, I ticked off the things I needed the manager to do. 'New carpets,' I said. 'Paint the walls, patch those holes and get me a quote for a new kitchen.'

'What for?', he exclaimed. 'Where will John [the tenant] keep his black crow if you carpet the lounge room?' He went on to explain how happy John was in his domain. He told me that John paid the rent, in person, at 4.10 pm every single Thursday, right after cashing his cheque and just before he headed to the pub. He also reminded me that the block on which these duplexes stood was huge, with development potential to build four new duplexes. He feared I would make John uncomfortable and cause him to leave before I was ready to develop.

Since that day I raised the rent on that property four times – in line with market sentiment but ensuring that I was not putting John in financial distress. The property has increased in value by 65 per cent. It has always had a positive cash flow. I have now torn down that original property and in its place stand four lovely new homes, and my cash flow has quadrupled. It sounds like the perfect investment, doesn't it?

I learned something from my experience. Not everybody wants what I want in a home. Smart as I may think I am, I *do not* have an instinct for what to buy. I *do not* know the needs of every market. Very possibly, the type of property I would personally prefer may be the type of property that is not in high demand as a rental. When I physically look at property, I either love it or hate it. If I love it, then I also want it. Not because it is necessarily a good investment, but because I just want it. As a result, I probably will not negotiate well, because I will be doing so based on my emotions. If I hate it, I will not consider it. I would not have considered the property that John rented from me, not in a month of Sundays. Yet as investments go, it has probably been one of the better of them, and it still has a long way to go.

BUYING WIDELY

I wrote the 20 Questions so you could buy property without allowing your emotions to interfere. By being commercial in your approach and buying property unemotionally, you also learn how to buy property widely, often in states in which you don't live. You might think that's not important, but read the following story about Tara and Chelsea and you'll see it is.

Example

Tara bought five properties in her home town at $300,000 each. She liked having them close by. She would drive by them on her way home from work every day to look them over and make sure the tenants were doing the right thing, so that she could attend to the matter straight away if she saw anything untoward. She may not have realised it, but she didn't get a lot of peace – she was constantly worried about these properties.

In year one, they each gained 5 per cent in value, so they were collectively worth $1.57 million. The extra $70,000 allowed Tara to buy another $300,000 property, and she again purchased in her home town, bringing her portfolio to $1,870,000. In the following year, the properties gained nothing at all, leaving the value at $1,870,000. She couldn't buy again, as she didn't have the equity.

The next year, she gained another 5 per cent, and so was able to add yet another $300,000 property to her portfolio. The portfolio now stood at $2,197,350 (the $1,870,000, plus 5 per cent, plus the new property at $300,000).

Chelsea also bought five properties for $300,000 each, each one in a different state. She saw returns in year one of 5 per cent on three of them, nothing on one of them and 2.5 per cent on the fifth, for total average growth of 3.5 per cent. At the end of year one, they looked like this:

1   $315,000

2   $315,000

3   $315,000

4   $300,000

5   $307,500

Her total increase of $52,500 meant she could spend only $250,000 on her next property, making her portfolio upon entering year two worth just $1,802,500.

243

In year two her properties had similar growth – three of them grew at 5 per cent (a different three, including the $250,000 property and the one with no growth the previous year), two grew at 2.5 per cent and one did not grow at all.

So, they looked like this:

1   $262,500 (the new property at 5 per cent)

2   $315,000 (the previously nil-growth property, at 5 per cent)

3   $330,750 (the property that grew at 5 per cent in both years)

4   $322,875 (the property that grew at 5 per cent in year one and 2.5 per cent in year two)

5   $315,000 (the property that grew at 5 per cent in year one and nil this year)

6   $315,187 (the property that grew at 2.5 per cent each year)

At the end of this year her portfolio was valued at $1,861,312. Total average growth this year was 4.16 per cent.

This additional $58,000 allowed Chelsea to spend $250,000 on another property, meaning she went into year three with property valued at $2,111,312. In year three, properties one to four went up by 5 per cent, properties five and six went up by 2.5 per cent, and property seven did not increase.

The values now were:

1   $275,625 (5 per cent growth)

2   $330,750 (5 per cent growth)

3   $347,287 (5 per cent growth)

4   $339,019 (5 per cent growth)

5   $322,875 (2.5 per cent growth)

6   $330,946 (2.5 per cent growth)

7   $250,000 (nil growth)

Average growth across the portfolio was 3.57 per cent. Her total portfolio at the end of year three was worth $2,196,502, and the increase in equity of $85,190 allowed her to add a property valued at $400,000. Her total portfolio after three years was $2,596,502. This is $399,152 more than Tara at the same point in time.

This example illustrates that spreading property over a number of different areas allows you to access differing growth levels at different times. This way, even in years where *some* of the property fails to grow, it will be rare for *all* of the property to fail. Important points to note are:

- Tara had considerably better average growth in two of the three years (5 per cent), but still came out behind in equity.

- Chelsea always had a property growing, and so was able to leverage every year into new property.

- Tara had to wait two years to buy another property, which meant she had less exposure to the growth market than Chelsea had.

- Even though Chelsea was getting lower average growth, she kept getting into the market again, giving her a broader base on which to obtain growth. Tara had higher growth but less property achieving it.

- The year that Tara had no growth could have been a great year for buying more property, but she had to miss out.

Being able to buy across many different areas is crucial for all property investors, both to add safety to their portfolio and to increase their exposure to different levels of growth. You would have to be one very unlucky investor to invest in lots of markets that all stagnate together. I have never seen it happen.

Buy widely, choose well and something will always be growing, which facilitates leveraging further.

SUMMARY

So, you can see that being commercial in your approach at all times is vital. Ask yourself if you are interested in a property because it has passed the test, or because you think it looks great. Ask yourself how you will feel if it all falls through and you do not end up with a purchase. Will you be able to walk away and feel nothing, or will it upset you? If it will upset you, then you have become too emotional, and you risk not doing your due diligence effectively.

We have literally dozens of properties, and very few of them are the types of property to brag about at parties. They aren't romantic, or attractive, or situated in areas where everyone wishes they could live. Nevertheless, there *are* dozens of them! I would rather have a large portfolio of properties in areas people turn their noses up at than one in an area that people are thrilled to hear about. We haven't bought these properties to make others envious. We have bought them because we are on a mission and want to be able to retire in a position that is better than we otherwise could have achieved.

So, keep your business hat on and put your heart in the drawer. Save it for family times, for birthdays and weddings. The 20 Must Ask Questions® will help you to do this. Not only will they increase your investing success and minimise risk as much as is possible (remembering it is impossible to remove risk altogether when you invest), they will also give you the confidence to buy property away from where you live without ever having to look at it physically.

Remember, while your eyes may not be doing the looking, your brain certainly is. Teach it to look deeply and, over time, you will succeed.

— Part III —

OTHER ESSENTIAL
INFORMATION

— *Chapter Six* —

GROWTH DRIVERS

WHEN YOU STARTED reading this book, you read about the debate that still rages between cash flow and growth investors. Despite overwhelming evidence that you don't have to forego one to have the other, we still see people confused about how best to buy property. The passionate growth investors who vigorously contribute to online forums insist that you should never venture more than 10 km from any capital city CBD, where high-priced, low-yield property can be bought in the hope that, over time, history will repeat itself and solid growth will occur. Conversely, those faithful to cash flow choose any property that can show them a weekly net positive cash flow, sometimes resulting in low-priced, high-rental-return property in regional areas and small towns where growth may be slower than in the city.

There are many problems with the growth-only approach. Firstly, it doesn't consider that those areas that may deliver great growth (such as those in big cities) fall the hardest when the market softens and can take years to recover. Also, as I have said, people buying only for growth can find themselves suddenly in a situation where it becomes difficult to add to their portfolio.

The high weekly commitment to the negative cash flow of the properties becomes more than they have available, especially if interest rates rise. The properties may indeed grow well, but the small number of properties owned (usually only one or two, depending on how negative the cash flow is) means that ultimately, their net worth is not as great as it needs to be to create a viable retirement income. Even a million dollars in equity will only provide you with around $50,000 a year in income. Add to that the fact that the negative cash flow along the way must be considered as a cost of the investment, and the total gain from taking a growth-only approach is often very low.

The trade-off a cash flow investor may make for being able to buy more property at a faster rate is a lower growth overall across the portfolio. If you use this strategy you can usually afford to add more properties sooner, due to the low or no cash input required – but if growth is too low, then leveraging into more properties using growing equity may be difficult or impossible. Your equity might only increase if you use the positive cash flow, and possibly extra cash of your own as well, to speed up the debt repayment.

So, it is important to adopt a strategy that will allow you the best chance of getting both growth and cash flow. You want to minimise negative cash flow and hopefully omit it altogether. You want your property to grow over time. The cash flow will get you there, the growth will keep you there and get you out when the time comes for you to retire. So, how do you achieve this?

As you can see from the previous chapters of this book, there is an abundance of research to be undertaken, whatever property or area you ultimately choose, and much of this research comes down to what I like to call 'growth drivers'. Understanding growth drivers, and knowing how to recognise and then assess them, may mean that you become an investor savvy enough to buy property that has a positive cash flow or close to it, but also grows well over time, increasing your net worth to the point where it can provide a viable retirement income.

I have written an entire book on this subject, entitled *Investing in the Right Property Now!* It is a really good way to get a deep and thorough understanding of what drives growth, and in turn you will become a better property investor. For now, though, it is enough for you to have an introduction to growth drivers, so read on.

WHAT IS A GROWTH DRIVER?

By reading this book and using it to buy an investment property, you have been collecting a lot of information about properties and applying the 20 Must Ask Questions®. In collecting this data, you have probably also uncovered many of the important growth drivers that determine the chances of the area growing consistently over time.

A growth driver is a factor that impacts positively on an area's ability to grow long into the future. Note that I have used the expression 'grow long into the future'. This is because much of the data you have uncovered so far will have shown that the area *can* grow. Whether it continues to do so is vitally important to you.

Past growth is not an indication of future growth, so property that is bought based on historical figures about an area's growth rates is not certain to grow. You also know from our discussion of trends that trends most often tell us where *not* to buy. In order to buy a property in an area that possesses all of the necessary characteristics for sustained growth over time, what you need to know is the difference between 'intrinsic' and 'extrinsic' growth drivers. Knowing this will help to protect you from choosing a property that fails to perform, and which subsequently leaves you unable to leverage into more properties (like Tara in the example in the bonus question).

EXTRINSIC GROWTH DRIVERS

Extrinsic growth drivers are the economic influences which contribute to the growth of an area, but which originate outside of that area as a result of influences occurring elsewhere. They are not a result of any micro-economic changes within that area; they come from activity, planning and events which occur temporarily.

When a large infrastructure project or a major building project is planned and executed in an area which has a smaller population, there is generally insufficient local labour available to fill the jobs which are being created. Often, workers will come from surrounding areas or even from interstate and, for the period of the project, they will be living in that area, most likely in rental accommodation.

This will place temporary pressure on many of those economic factors which normally result in property growth. The retail and hospitality trades will improve as these new residents spend what they are earning, injecting it into the local economy. Rental accommodation will experience short-term stress and vacancy rates will plummet. A knock-on effect will be house price increases – potential landlords witnessing the plunge in vacancy rates may see this as a sign of an impending house price boom and buy into the market, creating pressure on prices. The population is boosted by the new workers, often bringing with them their families, and the economy enjoys a burst of activity.

To the untrained eye, the features of a strong and growing micro-economy will be evident, and the temptation to get in quickly and on the ground floor creates a pseudo demand that can look like a true economic boom.

When the project completes, the workers move on to the next project, and the vacancy rates begin to rise. The funds which were being injected into the economy also dry up and many small businesses, which may have started up or flourished during the building of the project, close down. Pressure is removed from property prices and in fact prices drop as distressed landlords sell up. Often, values can return to 'pre-boom' days, and investors are left with property that is difficult to rent and hard to sell.

Similar results can come from other external sources. Pure investor sentiment, where the rumour is circulating that an area is heating up and investors from all over the country vie for a small pool of available properties, can create a short-term property demand which places a false reading on true house price growth. Equally, property developers who buy up cheap parcels of land, subdivide and then engage clever marketing companies to sell the properties – often to buyers from outside of the state – can also create an impression of potential growth which is never backed up by true economic vibrancy.

In the olden days, when computers took up an entire floor of a building and we got our news from the 6.00 pm bulletin, property investors traditionally bought property where they lived. The house next door would come on the market and the investor, thinking that it was time to consider their future financial needs, would see it as a good chance to begin asset accumulation. It made sense – they lived there and so knew it was a good area, and that the neighbours were decent people.

That in itself made it a good investment! Do you know anyone who bought property 30 years ago as an investment? You can be assured that almost all of them bought property only in areas where they lived. Successful investors owned the whole street and were none the wiser if their property performed better or worse than properties in another area, as this information was not freely available. We did not know what people were doing in other streets, let alone in other states!

Then along came the internet. Information about property anywhere in the country had previously been a scarce commodity, but suddenly it became possible to look at property, even take virtual tours, and buy it without ever making a journey. The landscape for property investment widened to include the entire country, and slowly more astute investors began to feel comfortable about investing sight unseen.

The next thing to happen was the discovery of positive cash flow property. It had always been known that some properties cost money each week and some gave money every week, but this new accessibility provided by the internet made investors more aware of just how possible it was to secure high-yield residential property in many areas around Australia. In addition to having a new consciousness of these higher-yield properties, they started to become more informed about how to use on-paper deductions to maximise their cash flow. Instead of waiting until the end of the year to visit an accountant and find out how much tax they could get back, investors were learning to assess property cash flows before they bought, and to make their tax claims every week as they earned their income.

What happened next? People began writing about it and shouting it from the rooftops. They were no longer content to make a retirement income for themselves from using these strategies: they wanted to make money on a grand scale, by selling the information wrapped up in clever educational packages. The market was flooded with books and seminars about properties purchased for extremely low prices with incredibly high yields in areas previously inaccessible to anyone but the locals.

During that time the claims were radical. There were reports of blocks of six apartments bought for sums such as $50,000, with total rent returns of $540 a week – giving stunning yields of 56 per cent per annum to those who had taken the 'risk' in country towns. Suddenly everyone wanted a part of that action. No longer was it acceptable to buy a few properties and sit and wait till retirement: you had to buy hundreds! Millions of dollars' worth! And they said you could do it all with no money down and no risk!

So, where were these properties? Why were they available at such low prices, with such high rent returns, and did they make viable long-term investments?

Example

Let's look at Kalgoorlie as a good example. Kalgoorlie is situated 600 km from the nearest capital city, which is Perth. The town has been built around the goldmining industry and essentially exists solely to house the miners who come to town to work their 14-day shifts, and then return for an extended break at their family home back in Perth or out of town. Since much of the town's population is itinerant, there is a very large demand for rental housing.

Prior to the advent of the internet there was, however, little demand for properties in Kalgoorlie. The people who lived in town were not interested in building a life there. There weren't many born and bred 'Kallies'. If you were in town at all, you were there for a reason. When a situation exists where demand exceeds supply, the basic laws of economics dictate that prices will rise. Demand for rentals in Kalgoorlie often exceeded supply, forcing rental returns upward. The supply of properties available for purchase often exceeded the demand from buyers, and so prices remained low. In short, we had a situation where the rental return on a property was well in excess of 10 per cent, giving a straight positive cash flow to investors without even the need to claim depreciation allowances.

When the search for positive cash flow property reached fever pitch, areas such as Kalgoorlie naturally saw a sudden inflow of investors.

The locals did not need to buy – people from out of town clamoured to be part of the action. This increased demand and decreased supply (because new properties were not being built and new land not being released) and had the inevitable result of pushing property values up very quickly.

However, there was not a related increase in demand for rentals. There was still the same number of jobs, the same number of people living in town and the same number of people wanting to rent. The rent values remained the same, so the yield on purchase prices began to decrease. Where early investors might have purchased for, say, $150,000 with a $300 a week rental return, new purchasers paid $400,000 for the same return, resulting in a negatively geared investment.

Things worked out well for those who got in early, because their yields were still based on their original purchase price. However, what did it mean in terms of sustainable investing? Would it work out over the long term for those investors?

What happened was this: the people who got in early had one boost in the first few years, when their equity grew as a result of the extreme interest from outside purchasers wanting the great yields. They were subsequently able to use this increase in equity to leverage into more property. They will continue to get a good cash flow on the original investment, which, if they are smart, they will use to repay debt and so create more equity.

However, since the growth drivers were extrinsic (from the outside investors) and ceased once the opportunity for positive cash flow diminished, future growth became limited. Kalgoorlie then faced an extended period of time during which little or no growth occurred. Kalgoorlie itself has little to stimulate growth – no increasing permanent population, no major infrastructure plans. Investment in the town slowed and those who already own property there will have to wait for rental yields to grow before investing in Kalgoorlie will be viable again, if it ever is.

This example, along with the stories of many other towns just like Kalgoorlie, shows that where growth is driven by extrinsic factors, positive cash flow investing may not be a viable way to build a substantial portfolio of properties.

INTRINSIC GROWTH DRIVERS

Intrinsic growth drivers, on the other hand, are the factors that affect growth that come from within an area. They include things such as population growth, demographic mix, accessibility to the area, proximity to a large centre or city and the local government's future plans for development, to name a few – in short, all of the things you have been finding out by asking the 20 Must Ask Questions®.

Example

Let's take, for example, the suburb of Mount Druitt in suburban Sydney. It is well outside the 10 km radius of the CBD, being situated 53 km west of the city. For many years, people considered Mount Druitt as housing a lower socio-economic group, and the values in the area moved incredibly slowly.

Ten years ago, it was still possible to pick up a three-bedroom home for just $345,000, with rent returns of around $400 per week – a rental yield of 6.02 per cent. In addition, there was an abundance of intrinsic growth drivers that told a story of viable future investing. The motorways had improved and provided much quicker routes into Sydney. The population was growing furiously due to the lower prices, and when the boom hit Sydney and made properties close to the city unaffordable to most, the demand in and around Mount Druitt increased even more. The prices more than doubled within the subsequent 10-year period.

Each and every one of these factors affecting this growth were long-term, sustainable characteristics that augur well for sustainable growth. Years ago, these characteristics were just as evident, and the prices were low and yields strong. Investors who took advantage of the market at that stage now find themselves with not only a strong rental yield, but also long-term, sustainable and continued growth.

What does this mean for you? It means that the property investment landscape is *not* painted with only two brushes – cash flow or growth. Investors do not have to choose between the two. It means that it is possible for astute property investors to seek out property that has strong rental returns and affordable prices today, and also has evidence of sustainable growth that will allow leveraging into more property. It means that cash flow investors must ensure that they do not simply buy because of the great returns, but satisfy themselves that there is every sign that their chosen property is in an area with intrinsic growth drivers. It also means that growth investors must accept that they can, in fact, move much further than 10 km outside a CBD and still obtain solid growth properties that may also have better than average yields. It is also acceptable to buy in areas that are unpopular with the locals. Remember my catchcry: *The locals can tell you the best area to live in, not the best area to invest in. They are thinking emotionally while you should be thinking commercially.*

You must understand that property investing is not just about growth. It is not just about the weekly cash flow or the success of the initial deal. It involves gaining a deep understanding of what drives a property towards future success, and doing an abundance of research to ensure that you can stay in the market over the long term. Your retirement income will be created by the net worth you can build between now and the day you leave work. Great cash flow without growth won't do this for you, but it may just keep you in the market until such time as you can finally afford to leverage into more property. Great growth with negative cash flow will mean that you cannot afford to buy enough to get the net worth you need, and if the economy turns against you and your costs blow out, you will be forced to sell before time. Owning properties that have both sustainable growth and short-term yields high enough to cover interest rate rises and vacancies will mean you have a solid, growing base of assets that will give you more choices in retirement.

— *Chapter Seven* —
THE BITS THAT DID NOT FIT

IN EVERY ONE of my books, the final chapter contains all of the bits that didn't fit anywhere else. In this case, there are not really any bits that didn't fit, as such. True, there are many, many things that I did not discuss, but that was because I have already covered them, sometimes more than once, in my other books. I wanted this book to be solely about the nuts and bolts of the research phase of buying property; it was not within its scope to cover what you have to do personally in the lead-up to buying, or how to buy, finance, settle, find management for and then oversee property on an ongoing basis. All of that information is important, but as I said, it is covered in my other books, which are widely available for purchase or to borrow from a library.

In this book, this last chapter is going to contain some of the really important 'bits and pieces' that have come up since I wrote my other books and I have not discussed anywhere else. Some of what follows are warnings about what to look out for; other parts are explanations of things people often asked me, which I clearly have not explained well enough before!

UNUSUAL FINANCING ARRANGEMENTS

Spruikers are wonderfully creative people. Just when I think that I have seen it all, a new guy jumps into the landscape with a remarkable new concept to help us all invest more profitably! At the time of publication, two new approaches to financing property have been invented over the past year or so, and I want you to be wary of them.

The first one is a mortgage that is marketed as being able to make a negative cash flow property into a positive cash flow property. Now, unless someone has actual magical powers, it is not possible to make a negative cash flow property positive unless you reduce your costs and/or increase your rents.

The spiel that advertises this loan, however, suggests that it can be done. This is how it is supposed to work. You apply for a loan to buy an investment property from this lender. As you are going to be offered a special method of repayment, you will borrow the money at a higher interest rate, say a variable rate of 8.5 or 9 per cent. To help you out, for the first year you may make repayments as if the loan was only at, say, 3.5 per cent. The unpaid difference between the two figures is tacked on to the balance of your loan. Each year, the rate on which your repayments are based is increased by 1 per cent. So, in the second year, your repayments would be based on a rate of 4.5 per cent; in the third year, 5.5 per cent, and so on. After five years, your actual repayment is the same as the applicable rate of the day. The marketing material claims that, as you essentially have a lower 'interest' expense, you can turn what was a negative cash flow property into a positive cash flow property – that is the magic part.

Let me spoil the fun and fill you in on the reality:

- The property is not really positive cash flow, as you are still being charged the entire amount of interest: you have just avoided paying some of it in the first few years. Cash flow is determined by income plus tax breaks, less expenses. Your 'expenses' are still the full amount of the interest charged. You are just deferring payment.

- There is an ongoing debate about whether or not you can claim capitalised interest on an investment loan. Some test cases prove you can, others prove you cannot. In short, the tax office disallows any claims on strategies that result in a personal benefit being obtained. This looks to me like a clear case of personal benefit – the money you would otherwise use to pay the interest bill on your loan is now being used for other purposes, probably as personal spending money or to repay personal debt! If you are told that an independent tax lawyer says that this strategy is legal and suitable, ignore it. Only personal rulings apply, so you would need to get a personal ruling on your circumstances to be able to legally use such a strategy. Since these sorts of loopholes are continually being examined and closed, if you are using one of these loans there is a high chance that you will not be allowed to claim the increased interest as a tax deduction in future years.

- This scheme relies on perpetually rising markets. You cannot predict future growth. If you don't get capital growth, you will end up with a loan higher than the value of property. You will have less equity than when you began, not more.

The second creative financing arrangement is not an invention or a new idea, but a fellow who tries to bamboozle investors by talking in circles. He appears at most major property shows and expos. I can best relate his particular idea with a story of how I found out about it.

A client of ours was at a property show and visited a stand that had property for sale at around the $800,000 mark. When she commented to the self-proclaimed expert that she would prefer positive cash flow property, he snorted at her. She asked him how much such a property would cost her, and he told her that it would be in the region of $300 a week negative cash flow.

When she enquired as to where she would get this $300, given that her family were young and they were living on one wage, he said, 'That's easy. You put a loan in place against the equity in your own home for the amount that you need to pay the first year's shortfall. [That would be $15,000.] It is like robbing Peter to pay Paul!' (Sorry, he didn't say that last bit. That was just what I thought when I heard it.)

She asked about the subsequent years. 'Well, you keep putting in a loan application each year against the increasing equity in your own home to cover the shortfall.' She told him that she thought the aim was to increase your equity, not continue to eat into it. 'You are not looking far enough ahead,' he said, and walked away from her (probably realising she was too smart for him!).

I explained to her that he was working on the impossible theory that property would go up by 10 per cent per year. Heaven help you if there was a real year in there somewhere – that would bring it all down like a house of cards.

The idea behind using property as your retirement strategy is to see your equity increase, so that one day in the future you can realise this equity and have enough funds to allow you to leave the paid workforce. You should completely reject any strategy that in any way requires capitalising loans, using equity to fund loan repayments, or in any way relies on growth every year to work well. You can only get ahead by working towards debt repayment so that you own your assets. The sooner you can pay off debt or reduce your loan to valuation ratios, the better.

PICKING THE BOTTOM

You've likely heard property spruikers telling you that it's 'not market timing', it's 'time in market' that makes property investing a success. As far as I am concerned, this is classic spruiker speak, designed to ensure that, once you have taken the bait and purchased from their stock on offer (and started to think that maybe you've been stitched up), you wait around for that magical 'time in market' to do its job rather than complain to them about the lemon they sold you. Eventually, most properties will grow and, if it's been long enough, you are less likely to do the calculations to discover that money in the bank would have been a better option for you than that property!

Another gem is that property 'doubles every 10 years'. At a recent property expo, I actually heard one presenter claim it doubles every seven years! He based the success of his own 'formula' on this assured doubling. It was easy enough for the audience to swallow that story, given that they all most likely lived in property in Sydney that had just gained about 70 per cent in three years. It was such an exciting time for Sydney property owners that most of those who had owned property longer than that had simply forgotten that for the years between 2003 and 2010 they were lucky if they saw a 17 per cent total improvement in the value. A doubling of value in seven years is going to be a real stretch even for those who got in just before this recent boom, and I can't imagine how people in Perth and Darwin would be feeling about that claim, given the sad performance of those two markets in recent years.

I've always said that, as long as you understand what drives property growth and choose property which possesses all of those characteristics, and then hold it for at least 10 years, you should, at some point in that 10 years, have a period of time when you do see a good spurt of growth – certainly enough to have made the buy worthwhile. I've also said that one of the most critical skills you need as a property investor is the ability to time your market well – good market timing every time you buy will absolutely improve the overall outcome of your portfolio. So it is understandable that everyone wants to know how to work out just when the market is at the bottom, so that they can get in to ride it to the top just before the tide turns!

It's important to note, though, that not every falling market will turn into a rising market, and not every market at the bottom will change direction and start to head to the top. If this is what you believe, then you could well find yourself with properties that sit in the doldrums for years, never showing any real growth during your investment period. It's highly possible for a property market to be low, and stay low, for a very long time, just as it's also possible for some markets to go up a little, then down again, then up a little, and down again, endlessly!

However, while it is actually not possible to pick when the bell is ringing to signify the turn of a market into an upward trend, there are definitely indicators that a market is trending up rather than down, and vice versa. Knowing what they are might help you pick better properties, avoid bad properties and divest properties that are about to head south, sooner. Here are some telltale signs that you can look for before you start to see an increase or decrease in actual prices:

- a shrinking of the number of days property stays on the market (or an increase, for a falling market)

- a reduction of the percentage by which prices are being discounted to effect a sale (or a rise, for a falling market)

- an increase in the rental yields when values aren't really moving yet (or a fall, in a declining market)

- a decrease to the vacancy rate (or increase, in a falling market)

- a short-term boost to population numbers which cannot be explained by other factors (such as large infrastructure builds bringing in new labour)

- a reduction in housing starts in the area (or an increasing number of new builds in a falling or stagnant market)

- a lack of new land supply (or an abundance of new land releases, in a declining or stable market).

While the above factors are not a guarantee of a market swing, up or down, being able to establish them will go a long way toward improving your property investing success. Identifying these factors requires you to carefully monitor the market and map the trends you see happening from month to month. This is why investing in hotspots carries so much danger – someone else has monitored the market and the upswing is already well under way by the time you hear about it!

Patience is the key, and knowing that there will always be a rising market somewhere should give you the confidence to wait and not jump in for fear of missing out. Conversely, don't use the need to monitor trends as an excuse not to buy if you're a procrastinator (read on for more about this) – take too long to establish whether the market is rising and you're likely to catch it while it's turning *the wrong way!*

REGULATION

While the buying and selling of property is highly regulated in most countries, and over-regulated in some countries, at the time of writing the *investment* property advising industry in Australia (and most likely in many countries) *is* still almost completely unregulated. You can sell Ugg boots at the market one week, and the next week you can be exhibiting at the property show and calling yourself a property expert.

It's little wonder that people make so many mistakes when they choose to invest in property! It is a minefield out there, and the opportunists are far cleverer than all of us put together. The Property Investment Professionals of Australia (PIPA), of which Destiny® is a foundation member, is still working very hard to lobby the government for regulation, and offers advocacy and support to investors in the meantime. The association provides a code of conduct and a set of standards for anyone working within the property industry today and has a good number of quality members. You can ensure you protect yourself by only dealing with property professionals who are members of PIPA, and making sure that your property adviser is a QPIA (Qualified Property Investment Adviser). Look out for further developments and find a qualified adviser by visiting www.pipa.asn.au.

HOW DOES IT END?

One of the worst things I find about many of the strategies being sold these days is that they all talk about the size of the portfolio you can build. It is always '$10 million of property' or '10 properties a year', and so on.

The problem with this, of course, is that these days, especially if you know how to borrow money repeatedly, *most* people may be able to 'have control' over $5 million of property. Unless you *own* some of it, however, it will do nothing for you! You could buy 50 properties, and they might even take care of themselves in terms of cash flow, but until you begin to own some equity in them, they are of little benefit: the cash flow is almost certainly too small to retire on.

For any strategy to work, it must have a clearly defined end point. You must know what your financial position is going to look like *at the end!* This way, you can also know when you will be able to retire.

When our Destiny® clients first meet with us, we prepare a projection for them. Not only does this projection identify how much property they can own outright (that is, without debt), based on what we know about how they earn and spend their income, we also project a possible retirement income for them, based on their return on equity. This way, they know when the amount and value of property they own will be enough to retire on.

By now, I hope you have worked out that I don't teach a get-rich-quick scheme. For some people, depending on the amount of income they have today and the platform from which they are starting (that is, how much equity they have now), it may not even be a get-rich-slow scheme! At the very least, however, it is definitely a 'retire better than you could on welfare' scheme, and for many it will be a 'retire a whole lot better than you could on welfare' scheme.

If you are looking for a strategy to make you untold millions, property may not be right for you unless you are in your early 20s. Property investing can set you up financially for the rest of your life, but it is not risky enough to catapult you into the world of the mega-rich. If, on the other hand, you simply want to have a better retirement, it may be perfect for you. To establish how much better your retirement income may be, consider the following calculations.

Assume that property, on average, yields around 5 per cent of its value in rent return. This takes into account the lower end at usually around 3 per cent and the upper at 6 to 7 per cent. If you are asking the 20 Must Ask Questions®, you are investing widely and so accessing differing degrees of returns.

Although you are probably paying the bank 4 to 5 per cent in interest, and you have other costs, you are also getting back tax on both the real loss and the on-paper loss, which will help offset some of these costs. That being said, the after-tax cost of any loans used for investing, plus the property expenses, will be around 5 per cent of the property's value each year.

Let's say you retired with $2 million of property, on which you owed $1 million. At a 5 per cent return, that would give you a gross income of $100,000 a year. However, you will have to pay out $50,000 of this income (5 per cent of the property's value) to support the $1 million loan and other costs: $50,000 remains yours. So, a $2 million portfolio with a $1 million remaining in debt should give you an income of $50,000 a year.

That is not millions, but if you have 10 to 15 years available and you apply all of these principles diligently, $1 million net in property equity may well be the least you will achieve.

Remember, too, that in retirement this $50,000 will be tax free, you will still qualify for some welfare assistance in many countries, your personal costs are likely to be lower (since the kids will have left home) and you will probably have no debt.

If you want to be earning more than this, you must aim higher. You will need more than $1 million of net assets. At $2 million, you can double your income to $100,000, and so on.

Imagine if in the first five years you accumulated $2 million of property with $2 million of debt. If we assumed a growth rate of, say, 5 per cent per annum, after five more years it would be worth $2,552,563. Five more years after that it would be worth $3,257,789. At that stage you most definitely would have paid off some debt, and your net worth would be somewhere around $1.5 million. At 5 per cent this provides you with $75,000 per annum in income.

From here you need to do some calculations for yourself, to work out how much you need to achieve in your first five years. Working on the basis that the bank will give you a loan of $5 for every $1 of equity (subject to serviceability criteria being met), you can also work out where you can start, given the equity you have in your own home now.

EVEN BETTER NEWS

You may be wondering why I haven't discussed selling down your property portfolio upon retirement and investing it in higher return asset classes. There are two reasons.

Firstly, upon retirement most people generally look at putting their savings into lower-yield investments, as they need to preserve their capital when their earning capacity is reduced. It seems silly to sell the accumulated property and pay the capital gains tax only to invest in another area with a similar return, unless you are realising the cash for something like a holiday or a new home for yourself.

The other reason is that property does something pretty nice that I really like – it keeps growing. While not all property grows, you have done your best to choose property that has every chance of growing and working out well for you by using the 20 Must Ask Questions®.

Say you retired at 55 with $1 million in equity on a $2 million portfolio ($50,000 a year in income at 5 per cent return). If you held on to your property for 10 more years and achieved a 5 per cent per annum growth rate, it would become a $3,257,789 portfolio. With a $1 million debt, there will be $2,257,789 in equity, and an income of $162,889! By the time you are 65, you will have tripled your income. Even if the growth rate were lower than 5 per cent, you would still increase your income. The property keeps paying for itself, and while that may mean you only take home the income from the part of the portfolio that you own outright, the increase in equity still occurs on the whole portfolio! That's not too bad, is it?

PROCRASTINATION

I get the chance to speak to a lot of property investors all the time, and I think I know how many of them tick. Often, it's at a seminar that I meet them, and they leave so full of excitement and determination – ready to go and get started straight away!

You might identify with this. Most likely you've been to a seminar or read a great property investing book and started planning what to do next. Some people make a firm commitment to get right into it and finally start investing, others plan on how they can expand their existing portfolio. All in all, there's usually excitement in the air and a conviction that action will follow.

The next day at work the excitement continues at least until morning tea time. Colleagues are apprised of the situation, the great seminar which had provided the motivation to take the future by the horns.

By noon it becomes apparent that enough time has been spent on excitedly imagining the future as a die-hard property investor and work needs to become the focus. By this time, you might have even looked at real estate websites and considered hotspots.

Come Friday night, the exhaustion of working so hard kicks in and all you want is a glass of red and to sit in front of the heater watching The Voice. Tomorrow you'll get into it.

Saturday dawns and you have things to attend to first: clean the house, mow the lawn, get the kids to and from sport, go shopping, call your mother, put on a load of washing. By afternoon you haven't stopped, so it's time to sit for a little bit, you'll switch on the computer later and get started on the big dream of owning a swag of investment properties. There's plenty of time. You can even start tomorrow.

Sunday arrives and – well, it's Sunday, it's your only real day off so you're not even going to go near the computer. Instead you read the paper. There's news that interest rates might rise and that the property market looks set to be affected. Mmmm. That's okay, it's only one report, but probably lucky you haven't done too much work yet.

On Monday morning, someone enquires whether you have bought a property yet, referring to that latest news. When you say, 'No, I was busy on the weekend,' they say, 'Maybe a good thing.' None of the agents have got back to you about your enquiries anyway, it just shows how hard this whole thing is going to be if you can't even trust those in the industry. The ball is in their court now anyway – what can you do but wait until they phone you?

Deep inside your mind that little voice (the one you call reason, but which in fact is really called roadblock) comforts you with comments like, 'You're not really ready yet,' and 'It's a big step and you're not really equipped, you should wait until you know more,' and 'You could lose big time here so you really should wait until the news is better/the property market is booming/you have more money/pigs fly/hell freezes over.' Yes, that feels better – you've made a decision and you're sticking to it.

Until the next year, when you go to a seminar again and you get fired up again, only by then you also kick yourself for not taking action sooner, because you can see the bargains you missed and the people who went home after last year's seminar and who, tired as they were, got on the internet that night and found their first, or next, property and, despite being busy/ tired/overworked, killed themselves making it happen because they did not want to be in your position next year!

Does this sound like you? Which person are you? Are you the person who, despite an impossible workload, too many commitments, lack of knowledge and still with a degree of uncertainty, decides that now is the time and you will not stop until you own a property?

Or will I see you next year, head hung a little as you tell me how excited you were last year but how life got in the way and you just couldn't take action. The time wasn't right. The planets just didn't align.

It's so easy to find an excuse not to get started, but much harder to find an opportunity to get into it. Your first (or next) investment property isn't going to come knocking on your door, and building a portfolio isn't going to come without challenges, drawbacks and risks. Retirement, however, will be on your doorstep in the blink of an eye and by then it will be too late.

So, what are you going to be doing this Saturday?

STAYING MOTIVATED

People from all over Australia have become clients of Destiny®. They are now enjoying an enhanced service provision that offers a top standard of support no matter where they live. These people have access to all of the information and knowledge that is contained in this book, and more that we present to them via the Essential Property Education Course, one-on-one meetings, client exclusive webcasts, Cloud Room sessions and more. However, we have discovered that it is not the information that makes people successful. I could write a thousand books and most people will still not make it work.

What makes it work is the support and motivation you get from others, along with a commitment to a system that requires you to attend to your strategy on a regular basis. Some of our clients have almost as many properties as we do, but they keep coming back to us, because they know that the support and motivation, as well as the specialist property investor tools we provide, are what keeps them going.

I am one of the lucky ones. I get to eat, sleep and breathe property investing. I work with it every day. I talk about it 10 hours a day. Of *course* we have a lot of properties – I just can't keep away from it! I do a seminar, and I motivate myself so much that I have to go home and trawl the internet!

You probably do not have that luck. You get small shots of motivation – from books, from seminars and shows – and then you go home and life happens to you. The kids get sick, there is a problem at work, and soon your good intentions have gone by the wayside until the next event picks you up again.

Successful property investors recognise the value of motivation and support and of using a system, and seek these out whenever they can. They realise that the chance to simply be around property investors and talk about investing is another chance to reinforce that what they are doing is right and they are not alone. People just love our group work because they get to meet with others just like them, every week. And it works. Find someone who can motivate you; someone to share your passion, pick you up and dust you off when things get hard and there seems to be no property left on the earth! Use a system that allows you to manage your loans and properties every week, so that they remain in the forefront of your mind and you think about them all the time. This will provide internal motivation for you.

And never give up. I mean, what else are you doing with your time?

YOUR PROPERTY RISK PROFILE

The following questions will help you identify your risk profile as it applies to property investing. Select one answer in each section and calculate your score at the end.

Select one answer for each question and calculate your points at the end.		
How would you describe yourself?		
Retired and dependent on existing funds/pension for income.	○	**1**
With a family to support. While you understand the need to invest, you cannot see how it will be possible, as your income is fully committed to the family budget.	○	**2**
Easily managing your current financial commitments. Your current income provides an acceptable lifestyle. Just starting out on your career or well-established.	○	**3**
At the peak of your career and income, possibly with a dual income. You have no dependants or easily manage the expense needs of your dependants.	○	**4**
What is your understanding of property investing?		
Not very familiar with it.	○	**1**
You understand the need to invest but no more.	○	**2**
You understand how different property types produce differing income and growth, and therefore have differing taxation implications.	○	**3**
You are an experienced investor with a current portfolio.	○	**4**
What are your financial goals?		
Income from an investment is the most important thing to you.	○	**1**

Safety is the most important feature for you.	○	2
You have a specific time frame of, say, around five years and a set return you would like to achieve in that time.	○	3
Growth is the most important thing to you.	○	4

If property were to lose value by 25%, what would your reaction be?

You would sell up immediately and never invest again.	○	1
You would keep what you had but not buy again.	○	2
You would be concerned but would wait and see for a while before you invested again.	○	3
You would not be concerned – you might even invest more while you can get a bargain!	○	4

Which do you prefer?

Stable though low returns.	○	1
Consistent returns with minimal tax savings.	○	2
Variable returns with good tax savings.	○	3
Higher returns with maximum tax savings (higher risk).	○	4

When do you plan to retire?

Already retired.	○	1
Within five years.	○	2
In five to 15 years.	○	3
In more than 15 years.	○	4

How often would you sell your property?

Never.	○	1
Within 10 years.	○	2
Every time there is a substantial gain.	○	3
Every year or two.	○	4

In relation to buying property unseen, you feel:		
You simply could not do it.	○	**1**
You may be able to do it if you had lots of pictures.	○	**2**
You would be happy to do so if you had someone you could trust to go and look at it.	○	**3**
You don't need to see it if the figures stack up.	○	**4**

Your score

This is a true and accurate reflection of my/our property risk profile.

Client 1 Signature _____ date _____

Client 2 Signature _____ date _____

QPIA® Signature _____ date _____

YOUR RESULTS

8 – 12 points: Conservative

Preserving your capital is the most important consideration for you. You have a short-term investment period in which income and capital stability are of prime concern. You should invest in low-risk property which includes standard residential property in well-populated city suburbs or large regional towns. You should ensure a low loan to valuation ratio (LVR) of <60%.

13 – 20 points: Stable

Your investment term is three to five years, and you are willing to take a small degree of short-term instability if it means the chance of long-term returns. Security is very important to you, and income is more important than growth. You could invest in standard residential property, with the option of smaller towns with economic vibrancy. You are comfortable with up to 80% LVR.

21 – 28 points: Balanced

You have a relatively long period in which to invest and are comfortable with short-term volatility for long-term growth and income. That is, you would like some security but are prepared to take some risk.

You could invest in standard residential, short-term holiday lets and some smaller commercial premises. LVR up to 85%.

29 – 32 points: Assertive

You look for growth and are willing to speculate. You can cope with negative returns and increased volatility. Growth is your prime concern over cash flow. You can consider most property and are willing to try niche-market, one-industry towns and all types of commercial property. You can manage a higher LVR up to 90% and negative cash flow.

ABOUT DESTINY®

FREE STUFF

Newsletters

Each month Margaret provides a free newsletter to subscribers, and once a week Destiny updates all subscribers with the latest property news.

Simply visit www.destiny.com.au/VIP and become a VIP – it's free!

Educational content

After years of educating property investors, Margaret has an impressive array of educational videos, podcasts and TV shows available for all property investors to access, free of charge. There are many ways that this information can be accessed – directly through www.destiny.com.au, via iTunes podcasts and video-casts, using your favourite Android podcast app or via www.destinylive.com.au, where a free subscription gives you access to a wide range of handy property investment tools and calcula-tors, as well as access to Margaret's complete knowledge base of videos. If you have a question about property investing, you'll probably find it by doing a simple search of that knowledge base.

Social media

You can follow Margaret on social media:

Facebook: Margaret Lomas
Twitter: MargaretLomasAU
Instagram: Margaret Lomas Property.

Also be sure to like our Facebook pages:

Destiny Financial Solutions
My Property TV.

Television shows

You can watch Margaret as she hosts Property Investing Matters every week via web TV at www.mypropertytv.com.au. It's a free show where each week Margaret hosts the top property investing experts from all over Australia, answering viewer questions and covering important topics.

PROFESSIONAL ASSISTANCE

Destiny Property Investment Services

After more than 25 years of helping thousands of investors to invest safely and successfully, Destiny has crafted a range of services to suit every property investor, from those just starting out on their property investing journey, right through to experienced investors wanting to add to or fine tune their property portfolio.

Utilising Destiny's vast experience, and under the guidance of Destiny founder Margaret Lomas, Australia's most respected, trusted and experienced property educator and commentator, Destiny's services will assist you to secure the financial future you desire.

So whether you are a novice or experienced property investor visit www.Destiny.com.au or www.DestinyLive.com.au to find out how Destiny can take you from where you are today, to where you want to be, using some or all of the following services:

Destiny Property Investor Education

If you're a do-it-yourself investor, or just starting out and want to become educated, then Destiny's Property Investor Education is perfect for you. It includes everything you need to become a savvy property investor, without all the extras that you may feel you don't need. Destiny's comprehensive property investor courses cover every single facet of property investing, from the moment you have decided to start or continue your portfolio, right through to the weeks after your new property is tenanted. Online and fully interactive, interesting and fun to undertake, we confidently say that no other courses prepare you so completely to tackle the challenges and rewards of being a property investor, and best of all, all our courses are written and presented by property expert Margaret Lomas.

Destiny Property Investment Plan

Do you want to build an individualised plan for your property investing future, to see what you as an investor can achieve? Do you want to set achievable property acquisition goals and see how future factors may affect your investing strategy, so you can make decisions accordingly? If this is you, then Destiny's Property Investment Plan is for you! After collecting information from you to be sure we tailor your investment plan to your individual needs, you'll have a session with one of our Qualified Property Investment Advisers where we will analyse your current financial situation, and using current market conditions and any future factors, create a blueprint of what you can expect to achieve in the amount of time that you have available to put together a portfolio. Best of all, your property investment plan can evolve with you on your property investment journey, so you will always know where you are, and where you are going!

Destiny Property Analysis

Do you want to get serious about investing and buy one to three properties in the next six months, but don't have a lot of time available to you? The Destiny Property Analysis service is for those investors who like to have some involvement but don't have time to do the detailed due diligence essential for safe and successful property investing. Once you've narrowed down a property, Destiny will complete a Property Analysis Report so you can be sure you know everything about the property, the area, and whether you are able to access finance for the property, before deciding to proceed. From valuations of the property's market value and its expected rental return, to calculating the individual cash flow of the property, our analysis will not only ensure you know the property intimately and have all the information you need to negotiate the right price, but also critically know how the property investment will affect you financially.

Destiny PropertyMatch™

If you are ready to dive straight into sourcing your next investment property, but just don't have the time to devote to the research and due diligence, then why not let the people who have been in the property investing business longer than any other company, and who have the most comprehensive expertise, help you? After building your individualised Investor Profile, Destiny will use the proven 20 Must Ask Questions® and proprietary PropertyMatch™ tools to identify the area, short-list properties, and formulate a property acquisition strategy most appropriate to your individual Risk Profile and financial circumstances. Once the property has been successfully negotiated, Destiny will manage the finance setup and the all-important structuring, and ensure a smooth run to settlement. But our service doesn't end there; we'll also assist with post-settlement activities and prepare a strategy for your next purchase. Destiny PropertyMatch™ is not only unique and all-inclusive, but the best value on the market, so you'll never have to pay a buyer's agent fee again!

Destiny Finance and Portfolio Monitoring

Whether you have a small or large property portfolio, or are just starting out, most investors don't have the expertise to source, set up and monitor their finance structure, or the time and tools to effectively monitor their growing property portfolio, potentially costing them thousands of dollars in lost rent, missed tax deductions, higher interest rates and finance costs, and missed investment opportunities. Destiny's Finance and Portfolio Monitoring will not only monitor your rentals to ensure they are at market price and increasing as they should, but will monitor your finance structure and the changing market conditions so you know when you are in a position to invest again, and can be confident that you are always in the best finance products available ongoing. And with more than 25 years of experience and billions of dollars in finance applications completed, you can be sure you are in safe hands with Destiny!

Also by Margaret Lomas

Investing in the Right Property Now!

How to Achieve Property Success

The Truth about Positive Cash Flow Property

A Pocket Guide to Positive Cash Flow Property

How to Invest in Managed Funds

How to Succeed in Property Negotiations

INDEX